No
Mountain
Too High

No Mountain Too High

Gladys Aylward

Myrna R Grant

CF4·K

Copyright © 2003 Myrna R Grant
This edition printed 2003.
Reprinted 2004, 2007, 2010, 2013 and 2017

Paperback ISBN: 978-1-85792-594-4
epub ISBN: 978-1-84550-883-8
mobi ISBN: 978-1-84550-884-5

Published by
Christian Focus Publications,
Geanies House, Fearn, Tain, Ross-shire
IV20 1TW, Scotland, U.K.

www.christianfocus.com
email: info@christianfocus.com

Cover design Alister MacInnes
Cover Illustration Norma Burgin
Thinking Further Topics:
written in-house by editorial team
© 2003 Christian Focus Publications

Printed and bound by Nørhaven, Denmark

To Anita,
who rivals Gladys in missionary zeal and
whose laughter brings out the sun.

Contents

Contents

Introduction

"What's the use of reading about a dead missionary?" Victoria plunked down on the sofa and eyed the small book her mother had given her. One of the best things about Victoria was that she usually said exactly what she was thinking. Her mum sighed. Sometimes it was one of the worst things, too. Her mother was sitting beside Victoria. She looked at her daughter lovingly. Victoria's dark hair was brushed back from her face and tucked behind her ears. Her hazel eyes challenged her mother as she waited for an answer. Instead of answering, her mother asked, "What sort of book do you like to read?"

"Well, about girls and their problems and their friends and the fun things they do and their adventures. Mysteries and exciting things."

Her mother took back the book on Victoria's lap. "Of course! This book wouldn't do at all!"

Victoria looked dubious. "Well, what's it about, anyway?"

"It's about an English girl who had many problems and longed to travel to the other side of the world, and lived a life filled with excitement and danger and who had one adventure after another. She was amazingly brave and a bit stubborn. Maybe like a certain girl I know."

Victoria grinned and made a face.

"– and she ended up famous and a Hollywood movie was made about her."

Victoria looked sceptically at the book, and then at her mother. "Mum — you're making this all up."

It was her mother's turn to grin. "Maybe I am and maybe I'm not. But right now I've got things to do." She stood up.

Victoria stood up also and pushed a dark strand of hair back behind her ear. "Well, let me look at it, anyway."

Her mother shrugged. "Suit yourself. But it is about a dead missionary!"

Victoria plopped back down on the sofa, tucked her legs under her and curiously opened the book. She began to read the story of Gladys Aylward.

A Rich Man Asks a Question

Gladys stood at the door of her employer's beautiful library. From the carpeted floor, bookshelves on three walls of the room climbed to the ceiling. Every shelf was filled with orderly rows of expensive volumes. Gladys' heart was beating rapidly and she hoped the guilt she felt didn't show on her face.

"You wanted to see me, Sir?" Gladys made a small curtsey as she had been taught. She was an experienced parlour-maid, and she knew the rules well.

"Yes, Gladys, please come in." Sir Francis Younghusband was a well-known army officer and explorer, accustomed to examining curious findings. Gladys stepped inside the room and closed the door quietly behind her.

"Now, Gladys, it seems you have taken a book or two out of my library." His inquisitive eyes studied how small a person this parlour-maid was.

"Yes, Sir. I'm very sorry, Sir. I really ought to have asked. But I put them straight back when I finished reading them. I *am* sorry, Sir." It wouldn't do to be discharged from her work.

Sir Younghusband smiled. "Now which books in *my* library might you be interested in?"

"Oh books about China. Sir!"

"China? And why China?"

"Oh, Sir, because I'm going to China as a missionary as soon as I can!"

"Is that so? Indeed! I've been to China, you know. Mostly India and Tibet, of course. Met the viceroy and the Dalai Lama. But China, too. It's a very long way from England, Gladys."

Gladys' face was alive with interest, her guilt about the books forgotten. "Yes, Sir. But as soon as I save enough money, I'm going!"

"All by yourself? "

"Not exactly, Sir. God will be with me."

"Yes, yes, of course." Sir Francis lifted his pipe from the mantle of the fireplace and took his time lighting it. A bit playfully he asked, "I hope you don't get seasick Gladys? It's a long time on the sea."

"I can't afford a sea voyage, Sir! I'm going overland by train on the Trans-Siberian Railroad. It's the cheapest way, so I can get there sooner. Every week I take as much of my wage as I can spare to the company as a down payment on my ticket."

For the first time Sir. Francis looked as if he began to believe that Gladys was actually serious. "Gladys! You can't just go off to China like that, you know. There's fighting on the border. The Japanese are invading China. The Chinese communists are marching against the Chinese government. It's very dangerous my dear, and you might not get back."

Gladys smoothed her apron and glanced down for a moment. When she raised her eyes he could see determination. "Oh, but Sir, I'm not *coming back!*"

The chiming of the mantle clock startled Sir Francis almost as much as her words. He had become so absorbed in questioning his remarkable parlour-maid that he had forgotten the time.

"Gladys, I have an appointment."

Gladys curtsied again and turned to leave.

"Gladys." He cleared his throat. "Uh, Gladys, you are very welcome to borrow any book you like from my library as long as you are careful and put it back where it was."

"Thank you very much, Sir."

"We will talk again about this matter. I can see that you are quite serious about your plans and that's commendable. But I think you do not know Chinese?"

Gladys nodded. She did not know one word of Chinese.

"And you are not trained theologically?"

"No, Sir. I applied as a missionary-trainee at the China Inland Mission and they said I was too old for studying and not clever enough to learn Chinese."

Sir Younghusband tapped the tobacco out of his pipe and shrugged on a nearby jacket.

"Yes, well, Gladys. Don't you think perhaps you ought to consider the advice of those older and wiser than you?"

"Not for a minute, Sir! I know what they say is true, but God says to go. So I ought to go, oughtn't I?"

Sir Francis paused at the door and took a long and thoughtful look at Gladys. "I'm an officer in the British Army, Gladys. I know how to give orders and how to obey orders. If you know that God has told you to go to China, then you'd better go, hadn't you?"

"Yes, sir." Gladys smiled as she retreated out of the room and closed the door behind her.

Gladys Has a Daring Escape

As much as Gladys had always enjoyed dramatic scenes, saying goodbye forever to her mum and her sister, Vi, at London's Liverpool Street train station had been almost too exciting. They thought they would see her again, but Gladys knew better. Once she got to China, that was it. She would make her life in China. She had given her mum an extra long hug and promised again she would write home as often as she could.

What a thrill she felt when the train gave off a huge chug, a powerful release of steam and a whistle blast to signal its departure. Now, huddled in a window seat with her two suitcases, Gladys tipped her foot on the pot and kettle she had tied to the handle of one suitcase to keep them from rattling together as the train jostled along. The "kettle" suitcase was crammed with food for her journey: tea and Ryvita, hard-boiled eggs, and fruitcake, the other, her few clothes, a blanket and an old fur coat someone had given her.

Hadn't God already proved to her that she was obeying His call? Imagine hearing about an old Scottish lady missionary in the remote north eastern part of China who needed an assistant! Hadn't God told her exactly where to go when she got to China?

The lovely English countryside in its autumn colours streamed past her window. It seemed no time until the train reached the English Channel and the special train that would be ferried across the water to Holland. From Holland, to Berlin, then on to the far-eastern port city of Vladivostok where she would begin what she thought of as her *real* journey on the Trans-Siberian Railroad to China.

"You go *where*?" The warmly dressed man with the heavy foreign accent had boarded the train in Warsaw. He looked at Gladys in disbelief. "All alone? And you go to China?"

Gladys nodded happily. "I change trains in Moscow to Vladivostok. "

"You alone in Russia? No one help you? "

Gladys smiled at the man's concerned expression.

"It very bad in Russia. You know Revolution?"

Gladys knew that the Communists had taken over Russia a few years ago and that they didn't believe in God.

"Yes, I know. I'm not staying in Russia. I'm going to China."

"You hope." The man shrugged before settling himself for sleep. "It very bad in Russia."

Gladys felt the cold seeping in from the connecting doors of the train. As they moved slowly south and east across the vast reaches of Russia, snow deepened. The train was very cold and Gladys piled on her grey blanket and the old fur coat and huddled in the corner of her seat against the window. She was glad for her little prima stove. She made many cups of hot tea and ate small meals of biscuits and cake. She read her Bible. She slept. She exercised by walking up and down the train corridor. She knew the Trans-Siberian Railroad was the longest railroad in the world and that she would traverse the whole almost ten thousand kilometres of track. Days passed. She lost track of time and when the train pulled into the last stop, Vladivostok, she was colder than she had ever been, stiff from days of sitting and hungry. And she was thrilled. From this place she would leave Russia and be on Chinese soil.

She was unprepared for the shocking scenes that confronted her as she disembarked from the train, dragging her two suitcases and wearing the old fur coat. Unkept soldiers were everywhere, the straps of their guns slung over their shoulders. Some gnawed on chunks of bread they carried with them. Grim-looking people packed the platforms, huddling on the ground, dark bunches of misery. The squalor was appalling. Refuse was littered everywhere. In long, seemingly endless lines people were crowded together waiting for bread. The roads were dangerously full of ice-filled holes and dirty snow.

As much as Gladys tried, she could find no one who spoke English and could direct her to her train. Finally two rough-looking soldiers approached her. Unable to understand their shouted demands, she offered her passport.

"British Citizen," she insisted, pointing to the royal seal on the cover of her document. "British! To China! Train to China!"

The soldiers seized her passport picked up her suitcases and pushed her through and over the crowds. Men, women and children were squeezed together in every inch of space inside the station and outside for as far as she could see. At a small table in a side room the soldiers thrust Gladys into a chair and gave her passport to an untidy officer sitting at the table in his coat and hat against the bitter cold.

He studied the passport. "Ah, a machinist!"

Gladys was mystified. What could he mean?

"We need machinists in Russia! You stay! We give you good work."

"I'm not a machinist!" Gladys felt tired and irritated. She mustn't miss the train to China!

The officer pointed to her passport. On the line that stated her occupation, was the word "missionary." His stubby finger tapped the word insistently. "Machinist! Machinist! You stay. You build revolution."

"I am a British citizen. I am not a machinist. I must go to China! Where is the train to Harbin? Give me back my passport and my suitcases. *Train to China!*"

"No train to Harbin. Not possible. Line closed to Harbin. You stay here. Good place. Build revolution!"

"I will *certainly not* stay here! I paid for a ticket to Harbin. I must get to China!"

The officer gave a curt order to the soldiers who collected her belongings and hurried her out of the room and onto a filthy street that ran along the back of the station. Each holding one of her arms, they pushed and lifted her along to a tumbledown hotel on the corner of the station road. Inside they gave the hotel clerk instructions before leading her to a room so small it contained only a bed. Dumping her suitcases and papers on the bed, they left.

Time seemed to have stopped. Only the fading light that sifted into the room marked the hours passing. Gladys was numb with fatigue and fear. She prayed but her prayers seemed to dwindle into nothing. She absolutely couldn't think what to do. There was no electric light and as night fell the room became black and very cold.

Suddenly there was a knock on the door so soft that Gladys was unsure if she heard anything or not. The knock came again just as quietly. As Gladys opened the door, a person pushed into the room and shut the door. In a heavily-accented English she heard, "Leave Moscow tonight. If you wait until morning, you will never leave. Gather your things and come. I will take you to a boat that is leaving for Japan. Hurry!" The voice seemed to come from a young woman.

Blindly, Gladys felt for her suitcases and passport. "Why are you helping me? Who are you?"

"Come. There is no time."

The hotel was in total darkness. Not even a candle burned in the lobby as the two rushed into the frozen street. The bitter cold bit into her lungs and Gladys hobbled as fast as she could, her suitcases banging against her legs, gasping for breath as she ran.

They finally stopped at a dock. "There is the boat." The girl pointed to a small vessel.

"But I have no money," Gladys' lungs felt on fire.

"You are British. He will take you." The girl gave Gladys an urgent push. "Hurry!"

"How can I thank you?" Gladys pulled off her warm gloves. "Hear, please. Take these."

The girl grabbed the gloves. "Hurry!"

The girl had been right. The captain had looked at her passport and waved her on board. At first light, the boat moved slowly away from the shore toward its destination in Japan, but Gladys knew that God would guide her to China! Jubilantly, sitting cross-legged on the rocking deck, Gladys wrote of her escape to her parents.

"I thought I knew the value of prayer, but never as now. When everything seemed against me He was there ready to help over the difficult places and here I am safe and happy, just waiting to go on and would willingly go through it all again for the joy of knowing my Saviour as I know Him now!"

And Gladys would have much more to go through before the end of her journey.

Gladys Arrives in China

Gladys knew she was right about God's leading. It was, of course, a surprise to be getting to China by way of Japan! The ship made its long and certain path through the shallow sandy waters of the Yellow Sea finally to dock in the beautiful Japanese city of Kobe. To the north were majestic snow-capped mountains and to the south the blue ocean. There was a Japanese Christian Mission station in the city and Gladys lost no time in hiring a rickshaw. This rickety vehicle, pulled by a small trotting man, seemed precariously like a chair on wheels to Gladys and she held on tightly.

At the mission she was welcomed and given a blissfully hot bath and a clean white bed. After the best sleep she had in weeks, she got ready for the last part of her journey: a long steamer sea journey from Kobe. Some Mission people went with her to the ship, urging the captain to take good care of this small foreign lady in the days ahead.

There were no chairs on the Japanese ship. Passengers sat on mats on the deck floor. Gladys's back soon began to ache but she distracted herself from the discomfort by admiring the spectacular scenery of the distant coastline. The autumn chill had turned leaves a blazing red. The peaks of majestic mountains were dazzlingly white with snow. Pretty houses with curved roofs and gates that were hung with fluttering banners nestled in green hills.

On the third day, in the late afternoon, the captain hurried to Gladys. She must come with him before the evening light faded to the side of the ship where she would be able to see the coastline of China!

Gladys stared joyfully at the distant shore and turned a shinning face up to the captain. "Oh, Captain, my heart is already there in China! *Whatever* I find there, I praise God for His goodness in letting me come, and protecting me all this way!" She stood straight at the ship's rail until twilight fell and the light deepened so that nothing more could be seen except the brilliant stars that were thickly spread across the night sky above her.

It would be two more days before the ship docked at the great port city of Tientsin and Gladys finally put her feet on Chinese soil. She noted the time and date in her diary: 4:30 a.m. on the morning of November 11, 1932.

Gladys believed that Mrs Lawson, the old Scottish missionary she had come to help, would be eagerly waiting for her in Tientsin. Little did she imagine the scepticism with which Mrs Lawson had read Gladys's letter saying she would come. An English parlour-maid? Really? Come by herself to China? No mission society sending her and no money for her journey? Well, the girl probably *meant* well, but Jeannie Lawson wouldn't hold her breath! She certainly wouldn't make the long journey to Tientsin to wait for someone who was very likely never to arrive!

At the English-Chinese college in Tientsin, Gladys was close to tears as the kindly principal told her that Mrs Lawson hadn't been to Tientsin in a long time. Nobody was sure *where* she was, but the last they heard she was in Tsechow.

"Is Tsechow very far?"

The principal directed Gladys into the mission lounge where a steaming pot of tea awaited them.

"Do sit down and have some tea, Gladys."

Gladys sat. "Thank you very much. But Tsechow: is it very far?" Gladys sipped her tea gratefully.

"Gladys, it's in Shansi Province. It's very rugged, mountainous territory, but I can tell you how one would get there if you really want to do it."

Gladys was astonished. "But of course! I must get to Mrs Lawson. I've come all this way . . ." Was it the steam from her tea that was making her eyes water? "How far away is it?"

"You'll have to take a train to Peking. That's about 100 miles away, because you need to get the train there for Yutsu, which is a journey of about 250 miles. Unfortunately, Yutsu is the end of the railway line. From Yutsu you'll need to get buses south until you reach Tsechow."

Gladys cleared her throat and sat up straighter than ever. "How long will it take? I can't picture the distances."

The principal poured himself another cup of tea and stirred the milk in slowly before he spoke.

"I know how tired you must be Gladys. I'm so sorry to tell you that a journey like this, in China, will take two or three weeks at best, perhaps a month."

A month! Gladys said nothing. She suddenly felt very, very tired. She tried to imagine how she would manage travelling for weeks without one Chinese word to her name and with no one in the remote and wild areas who understood one word of English.

"And Gladys, we don't really know if Mrs Lawson is *in* Tsechow. That's only the last place we heard she was." Seeing Gladys's pale face he quickly added, "But people there will know where she is. She shouldn't be far."

Gladys finished her tea. She put down her teacup with a shaking hand.

"I thought Tientsin would be the end of my journey —" her voice faded out as she contemplated the ordeal ahead.

The principal stirred his tea sympathetically.

"You must stay here and rest while we try to find you a guide to take you into the interior. You are most welcome here."

After a minute Gladys stood up. "Thank you very much for the tea." She tried to smile but her heart was heavy.

"Right! I'll begin asking around and find you a guide."

"A guide. Oh, yes! That would be wonderful!"

"And now you must rest. Your journey won't be an easy one."

"None of them ever are!" Gladys thought. Gratefully she made her way to the guest room and slept.

Gladys Bursts Into Tears

After a restful week in Tientsin, a guide had been found. Yet again Gladys found herself and her two suitcases on a train swaying through immense stretches of countryside. But this time, she was in China! She loved the changing scenes that passed across the windows of the train: pagodas and temples, camel caravans, strings of mules so loaded down with burdens they could scarcely walk, coolies mincing along with carrying poles balanced across their shoulders.

When the train stopped for the night they stayed at Chinese inns so strange to Gladys she could barely sleep. There were no bedrooms, curtains, or even beds. Along one side of the wall was a raised brick platform heated underneath by a fire. Everyone slept, fully clothed, all together on the hard platform: men, women, children, government officials and peasants. The night was filled with muffled sounds: a baby's startled cry, gentle snoring, sleepy grunts, the clucking of somebody's caged chickens.

Gladys had been told that in Tsechow there was a church and a boarding school for children of Christian parents run by a kind British lady. It all sounded much more civilized to Gladys and she could hardly wait to get to Tsechow and Mrs Lawson. But Mrs Lawson wasn't in Tsechow.

Gladys stared at the genteel English missionary at the Tsechow mission compound. She had come out to China fifty years ago with her young husband, Stanley Smith, a graduate of the famous Cambridge University in England.

"Mrs Lawson is in Yangcheng, dear. It's not so far," she added quickly, seeing Gladys' dismay. "But it is very rough country. There are no roads over the mountains, you see, just caravan trails. But you'll get there, safe and sound, in two days' time. You'll have to travel by mule."

A mule! Well, if Jesus could ride a donkey into Jerusalem, she could ride a mule into Yangcheng. She was pleased by the idea. She was further pleased when Mrs Smith provided her with simple Chinese clothes.

"You can't travel in Western clothes now, dear. The Chinese don't like foreigners very much, I'm afraid. It's better to fit in as much as possible. You'll find that they will all call you 'foreign devil.' Don't take it at all personally."

Gladys promised not to mind. Privately she wondered how a person could *help* minding such an insult. But after a rest and the tender care of Mrs Smith, Gladys and her guide set out. This was the *real* China. Out in the fresh air, with the striking mountain scenery, this was *her* China! She patted her mule and was thankful for its sure footing on the narrow trails.

As the hours passed, Gladys became less thankful and more anxious for any stop where she could stretch her aching bones. But at last, on the second day they saw the walls of Yangcheng in the distance. No sight ever looked so beautiful to Gladys. Rising above the walls were wonderful buildings which Gladys thought came straight out of a fairy tale. The roofs were curved into storybook shapes with turrets and towers. Here she would begin preaching the gospel. After she learned Chinese, of course!

Her aches and pains were forgotten as they entered the city by the East gate and were directed to Mrs Lawson by a mule driver. Gladys noticed he stared at her in distaste but was so pleased to have arrived that she smiled at him anyway.

Mrs Lawson was a small, white-haired old Scot who also stared at Gladys as the mules entered her broken-down courtyard.

"Who are *you?*"she demanded.

Gladys was exhausted. "I'm Gladys Aylward." Without being invited, she got down off the mule. "From England," she added hopefully although England seemed as far away as the moon.

Mrs Lawson didn't look at all pleased. "You'd better come in then."

The house was even more broken-down than the littered courtyard and some boxes by a window served as table and chairs. The rest of the large room was completely empty except for the long brick platform along one wall that Gladys now knew would be the only bed.

"I got this house cheap two years ago," Mrs Lawson announced. "The Chinese think it's haunted." Mrs Lawson called something out in Chinese and immediately a cheerful man appeared. "Yang, my cook," she explained. More Chinese. "I've told him to bring you some noodles."

"Thank you." Gladys tried a smile. "I haven't really —"

"I've been in China fifty-three years. I'm seventy-three years old. What do you think of that?"

Gladys opened her mouth to answer.

"I have big plans for this place. We're going to turn it into an Inn. Get the Chinese muleteers in here. Give them a meal and before they turn in, the gospel!"

Yang set a bowl of hot soup before Gladys, filled with vegetables and noodles.

"Don't think you're going to live on rice in Yangcheng. There's no rice here. Shansi province is the gate to two of China's great wheat-growing provinces. Noodles. That's what we eat here."

"Thank you. It's very good." Gladys nodded yes when Yang offered another bowl.

"Put your things anywhere. Take a stroll if you like. Get the lay of the land. We'll start cleaning this place tomorrow."

This was not the welcome Gladys had imagined. Mrs Lawson had not so much as shaken her hand before going off to another part of the house. Still, Gladys comforted herself. She had safely arrived and in such a pretty place. A stroll before bed would be good. Full of curiosity, Gladys made her way out of the courtyard and into the street. Groups of women were carrying water jars along the road. They stared at Gladys. Well, of course. That was all right. They weren't really rude. She was still a stranger. Then the women lowered their water jars and scooped up clods of dirt and flung them at Gladys. They shouted at her: *"Lao-yang-kwei Lao-yang-kwei!"* A little crowd of children gathered, laughing and joining in.

At first Gladys was too surprised to move. Then she turned and fled back to the courtyard. The old lady hurried out to see what was causing the commotion. Gladys burst into tears.

"People threw mud at me, " she sobbed, trying to brush the dirt from her clothes.

Mrs Lawson nodded her white head. "Course they did, my girl. Happens to me every time I go out. Yangcheng is about the most unfriendly city I've ever seen in China. They call us foreign devils. Now stop crying. We won't save any souls with you crying at a little bit of mud. Get yourself some rest. Tomorrow we start work!"

Gladys climbed up onto the brick platform and pulled her old fur coat around her. It had been a very cold welcome!

Gladys Terrifies a Mule

Mrs Lawson was not one to suffer fools gladly and she soon let Gladys know she would stand for no nonsense and no objections to her plans. She would turn the broken-down mission house she had rented into an Inn for the mule caravans on their way over the mountains to Honan. It was a fine plan and they would have a captive audience every single night to hear the gospel.

Gladys knew all she wanted to know about Chinese Inns: dirty men, fleas, disturbances all night long, spitting, coughing and bad smells.

"None of *that*, my girl," Mrs Lawson's blue eyes narrowed in determination. "I am seventy-three years old and have been in China most of my life. Tried retirement at home, didn't like it, came back, paying my own way, too. I'm going to die in the saddle, giving the gospel to whoever I can. In this town, that means muleteers. The village people won't stop throwing mud at me long enough to listen!"

Yang stood by the stove, nodding his head in agreement although Gladys wasn't sure he knew a word of English.

"Yang can cook for the men. You can bring them in."

Gladys felt a shiver up and down the whole five feet of her small body.

"*I* can bring them in? I can't speak Chinese. And when I go out into the street people throw mud at me too."

"Nothing easier! Yang will teach you what you need to say. All you have to do is give a good pull on the reins of the first donkey, and if you get him in, the rest will follow, including the men."

Mrs Lawson gave a sudden grin and called out some words in Chinese.

Yang bowed vigorously in approval.

"We have no fleas! We have no bugs! Good, good, good! Come, come, come!" Mrs Lawson translated herself shouting the words in English with an exaggerated grin and bowing up and down energetically.

Gladys felt an urge to laugh. She looked at the ruin of the courtyard and house. She looked at the frail and elderly woman standing so defiantly before her. She thought of herself, a new missionary whose first words in Chinese would not be, "Jesus loves you!" but "We have no fleas!"

The next weeks were spent in backbreaking labour. For all her years, Mrs Lawson was a dynamo, sweeping away debris, driving nails into wobbly arches, pushing their little wheelbarrow time after time out of the gate and unloading its contents onto a nearby dump. Yang cut piles of firewood for the long brick stove under the sleeping platform and for his own kitchen stove, and carried in bales of hay for the donkeys. Gladys scrubbed every inch of the rooms with strong soap and a primitive brush until her hands bled. When they stopped for meals, Yang patiently taught Gladys the strange sounds of the Chinese phrases she needed to advertise the Inn. *Muyo beatcha! Muyo goodso! How, how, how! Lai, lai, lai!*

At last their opening day came. Mrs Lawson looked very pleased with herself and Yang looked mysterious. "What does he think of all this?" Gladys wondered. Two foreign devils, one a very old lady and the other a very ignorant young woman opening an Inn for the rough and dirty mule drivers that passed through Yangcheng? Yang merely bowed and nodded and said nothing.

As the light of their first day faded and the time for the closing of the gates of the city drew near, Mrs Lawson pushed Gladys to the entrance of the courtyard.

"This is when the mule trains come. They stop for the night and have to get into the city before the gates are locked. Out you go, girl!"

Gladys stumbled into the road and looked fearfully at a caravan of mules led by a ragged driver making their way into Yangcheng.

When the driver got almost next to her, Gladys took a deep breath and sang out the words Yang had taught her. "*Muyo beatcha!*– "The driver's eyes widened and his mouth opened in a terrified shriek. At first he fled down the road, leaving the mules in disarray. Then he rushed back on the other side of the road, leading the mules in a wild stampede to escape. There was pandemonium as onlookers dashed out of the way of the confusion.

Panicked, Gladys rushed back into the courtyard. Mrs Lawson, waiting, like a good Innkeeper to welcome her guests, was exasperated. "Silly girl! Don't just *stand* there when a caravan gets near. Of course the men will run away from you if you let them! I told you to get a hold on the lead mule and pull him *in*. The drivers will have to follow, don't you see? They can't lose their mules." She shook her head as if to say there was no one more useless in the world than a London parlour-maid!

Gladys wanted to plead with Mrs Lawson not to make her try again. She wanted to say she couldn't do it, that she was afraid of the mules and wild-looking men. That she *wouldn't* do it. In a sickening flash she realized she had no hope of escape. She knew Mrs Lawson would pay no attention to her pleas no matter how desperately she implored her. She knew, just as surely, that Mrs Lawson was getting ready to push her out into the road again.

Gladys lifted her chin and marched back to the gate. If she failed again, so be it. But she wasn't going to give up without getting one of those mules. This time she didn't yell. She stood quietly waiting just outside the courtyard until several caravans came jostling along the road. Quickly she seized the reins of a mule at the head of a line and pulled with all her might. The mule brayed piteously, flinging her forward as it reared back. Gladys hung on, the muleteers shrieked and with a mighty yank she got the mule through the gate. Mrs Lawson seized the reins and helped pull in the line of mules tethered together. The hay in the corner of the courtyard seemed to quiet the mules and they made their way across the courtyard quite peacefully.

"Well done, *Gladys!*" Mrs Lawson was breathless but she happily hurried to the small group of muleteers peering anxiously into the courtyard.

"Gladys!" Mrs Lawson pulled Gladys with her. "Go ahead!"

At first Gladys didn't know what Mrs Lawson wanted her to do. Then, seeing the faintly mischievous smile on her weathered face, Gladys bowed politely to the men. "We have no fleas. We have no bugs! Come, come!"

The men looked startled, then one laughed. They all laughed and the strained atmosphere was broken. Mrs Lawson busied herself bowing and explaining the advantages of their Inn. Gladys knew she would be saying, "Lovely noodles. Delicious soup. No fleas. No bugs. And after dinner, *stories!*"

Gladys Meets a Mandarin

The stories Mrs Lawson told at the Inn became very popular with the muleteers. Not only did they find Yang's food good and the Inn clean, but the strange white devil, helped along in her Chinese by the cook, never charged for the evening's entertainment and seemed never to tire of her tales of the miraculous Jesus and the wicked warlords that opposed him.

Mrs Lawson's great patience with the Chinese did not extend to Gladys. Her temper often flared for the smallest of reasons. Gladys learned to accept her tirades and simply wait for the anger to pass as it always did.

One day Mrs Lawson asked Gladys to come with her on a walk. Gladys was practising her Chinese with Yang. "Might I just stay here and go on with my Chinese?" she asked politely.

Mrs Lawson's face reddened in a way that Gladys had seen before. "Ah, I see! I am disturbing you, am I? I am interrupting what *you* are doing! You can't possibly spare a few minutes away from Yang for a walk with *me*."

Gladys rose to her feet. "Please don't be angry," she began.

"Angry, is it? Angry? And why should I be angry at you? I'm the one who is interfering with *you*! I should apologize for annoying *you!*"

Yang was slowly backing into the kitchen. Mrs Lawson's fury seemed to grow the more she expressed it. Finally, as a last volley before stamping out the gate she said, "And if you can't be bothered going for a walk with me, I can't be bothered having you around. I want you out. Get out, you and your suitcases, and go somewhere else to learn your Chinese!"

Gladys was stunned. Where could she go? Tsechow was two days' journey. She couldn't stay in the village. Yang patted her arm in comfort. Mrs Lawson would get over it. In a few days she would ask Gladys to come back. He was sure of it. Gladys could visit the mission in Tsechow. Yang would find a guide. All would be harmonious again!

So Gladys, with a heavy heart, set off for Tsechow. Mrs Smith at the mission station was delighted to see Gladys again and to hear of her adventures in Yangcheng. She too was sure Mrs Lawson would want Gladys back. In the meantime, Gladys could sleep in a real bed, drink tea from pretty cups and saucers and enjoy a rest. Gladys loved the gentle Mrs Smith and her unfailing kindness and beautiful manners. And Mrs Smith was right: Gladys *was* very tired. It would be very nice to stay for a little while and on Sundays to enjoy the proper Anglican Church that the mission had for local missionaries and Christians.

One morning as she and Mrs Smith were having their 11 o'clock tea, a messenger burst in. "A very old and sick foreign lady had been found on the mountains.

She was dying somewhere in one of the remote villages. He didn't know which village. What was to be done?"

Both Gladys and Mrs Smith knew it would be Mrs Lawson. Hurriedly they prepared Gladys for her journey to find Mrs Lawson. Food and water and some medical supplies were bundled together. A mule for Mrs Lawson was hired. A guide was found and Gladys set off in a fever of impatience, trying to hurry the plodding mules as they picked their footing along the narrow mountain paths.

On the fourth day of their search they came to the little walled village of Chin Shui. In answer to their routine inquiries, they got the answer Gladys had been praying for. Yes, there was a foreign devil in the Inn! She had fallen off a balcony and no one knew what to do with her. Go quickly to her because she might already be dead. Take the foreign devil away!

It was very dark in the Inn and the servants carried bobbing paper lanterns to where Mrs Lawson was lying. She was delirious and had many cuts and bruises from her fall. Gladys realized that she had done something serious to her back; every move caused her great pain.

"Oh, Gladys, Thank God it's you!" she murmured. "Take me back to Yangcheng. Take me home. I don't want to die here."

Where Gladys decided to take her, was to the hospital at Luan, where there was a European doctor. It was an agonizing journey of six days, with guides carrying Mrs Lawson on a litter. For several weeks

Gladys nursed the old woman who seemed to slip farther and farther away as the time wore on and her cuts and bruises healed. Whenever she was strong or clear-headed enough to talk, she begged over and over to go back to the Inn.

When nothing more could be done and the kindly doctor warned Gladys that death was near, Gladys sadly journeyed back with Mrs Lawson to Yangcheng and the Inn. There the faithful old missionary left this world for her home in heaven.

"Now what is to be done?" Yang bowed respectfully to Gladys. "The old one is gone. We have no money. Do we?" He looked hopefully at Gladys.

"No money," she agreed. "Mrs Lawson had an allowance from somewhere. That's how she kept the Inn going."

"You have such allowance?" Yang was always optimistic.

"No allowance. No money at all. Nothing. We can't even pay for the rent for the Inn or the taxes when they are due."

Yang looked thoughtful. "You must go to the Mandarin."

The Mandarin was the high public office that ruled the mountainous villages of southern Shansi Province in the name of their warlord and governor. Mandarins had absolute power over village life and people. He set the taxes and made all the laws. He ruled who would live and who would die.

"Whatever for? I've never even *seen* the Mandarin."

"It is a matter of respect. It is a courtesy."

"Courtesy or not, I don't know how to do it. And my Chinese isn't good. "

Yang couldn't argue with that. It was a dilemma and one Yang couldn't solve. He didn't know the protocol for a foreign devil woman to meet a mandarin, even if her Chinese were perfect.

He bowed sadly and went off to make the soup for the muleteers who continued to come, night after night.

The days passed quietly with Yang and Gladys establishing a routine that was easy to follow. There was no longer any need to pull the mules into the courtyard. The mule trains came eagerly, some nights as many as six or seven caravans crowded into the courtyard. Yang served the meal and after dinner, Gladys stammered through simple Bible stories, her Chinese improving as she went along. Sometimes she and Yang would sing hymns as a special attraction. Gladys was thrilled when Yang declared he wanted to be a Christian. Eager to share his new faith, there were nights when Yang himself told the stories. With the best of intentions, he invented fantastical tales of Jesus on the ark, Mandarin Moses on a throne, and the disciples walking across the river called Jordan. Gladys did her best to correct him when she understood what he was saying in his quick Chinese.

One morning there was a commotion in the courtyard long before the mule trains were to appear. Yang was shouting hysterically at the Gate, running back and forth from the Gate to the Inn, calling for Gladys. She stuck her head out of an upstairs window.

"Ahheee! The Mandarin is coming! The Mandarin is coming! Ahheee!" As soon as Yang saw that Gladys understood, he fled out into the road. Hours would pass before he ventured back to the Inn.

Gladys had never before seen a spectacle like the one that unfolded before her in the courtyard. There was a continuous tinkle of bells. And the shuffling of many feet. A sedan chair carried by four coolies emerged from the dust of the road. Its coverings were elaborately embroidered with brightly coloured birds, flowers, goldfish, cats and dragons, on shimmering silk. Around the sedan were gathered official-looking men in dark blue robes. As the sedan stopped, all its little bells were stilled. One of the officials stepped forward and opened the door of the sedan, bowing and offering his arm. All the men bowed deeply. The Mandarin emerged, resplendent in a robe embroidered in every colour of the rainbow and shot through with glittering gold thread. He was tall, with a whitened face and a drooping black moustache.

Gladys also bowed as respectfully as she knew how. For good measure, she bowed again. The Mandarin was silent. Gladys too was utterly silent. She couldn't think of even one Chinese word to say.

Finally the Mandarin spoke. What he said astonished her. Had she understood?

"I've come to ask your advice."

Gladys Unbinds a Tiny Foot

Gladys was frightened. How could she answer such a high official? She couldn't invite the Mandarin and all these long-robed officials into the Inn. Yet standing in the courtyard was awkward. Still, there was nothing for it but to do her best. Gladys took a deep breath. In the most polite way she could think of, she began.

"I am honoured, Mandarin, that you have come to my unworthy Inn and to my unworthy self. I am your most humble servant."

The Mandarin nodded gravely before he spoke.

"For a thousand years China has practised the ancient custom of foot binding."

A stab of alarm struck Gladys. Was he going to demand that her feet be bound, according to the custom? Gladys had seen the tiny, deformed feet of the village women as they hobbled to and from the well to draw water. She had seen the baby girls' feet tightly wrapped to prevent them from growing. She had heard their cries of pain from behind the walls of their houses as their mothers changed the bandages and wrapped the strips of cloth ever tighter around their poor feet.

"China has an honourable new central government."

Gladys nodded although she had heard nothing of any new government.

"The government has ruled that all foot binding of children must stop immediately. Mandarins across all of China are responsible for carrying out these wise and venerable orders."

Gladys nodded again. At least *her* feet were safe!

"I have given the order. But I must have a foot inspector to be sure this law is obeyed. This inspector must unbind the feet of the children if the mothers refuse. An official or soldier cannot look on a woman's foot nor unbind the feet of a small girl. I must send a woman. But what respectable woman could travel up and down the mountains, sleeping in Inns, away from the house of her husband and father? What virtuous daughter of China could be appointed? Not one."

"No, honourable Mandarin." Gladys was completely mystified.

"So I appoint you!"

The Mandarin looked very satisfied with his solution.

"You will carry with you my orders on an official scroll. You will be paid and I will give you a mule. I will send two soldiers with you as guides and for protection. You will go to every village and command the women to unbind their children's feet. You represent the Mandarin. If they refuse, their husbands will be sent to prison. The soldiers will see to it."

Gladys bowed deeply, too astonished to say a word.

"I am the Mandarin's insignificant servant," she finally managed. Well, she had been a parlour-maid in London. She guessed she could be a mandarin's servant in China!

The Mandarin turned. Leaning on the arm of an official, he parted the beautiful silk curtains and climbed into his sedan. The little silver bells tinkled as the sedan was lifted up by the poles onto the shoulders of the carriers and the procession slowly left the courtyard.

Paid! Gladys was in bliss. That would solve the tax problem! She could hire someone to help Yang with the Inn when she was away. And she could travel safely even along the most dangerous and remote mountain trails protected by the Mandarin's soldiers. And she could tell Bible stories in the villages and the people would not dare to throw mud or run away.

God had answered her prayers! He had made a way for her to take the gospel throughout the district. God had met her needs! And in such a funny way! Gladys would have danced back into the Inn but she was afraid someone passing would see her and would be convinced that the foreign devil was crazy!

Yang was impressed when he crept cautiously back to the Inn after the Mandarin had gone. Gladys was no longer only a foreign devil. She was a servant of the Mandarin himself! And Yang was a servant of the Mandarin's servant! He lifted his chin in pride. This would make their Inn important once people knew of the great honour that had been bestowed upon the foreign devil. Good fortune had smiled on them.

Early the next morning, in the dawn drizzle, a few roosters were scattered by the sudden appearance of three mules and two soldiers. Gladys had risen before the first light and was ready. After a hurried goodbye to Yang, she mounted her mule and the little official troop briskly made their way to the city wall as the gates were unlocked and heaved open.

It was the happiest Gladys had been since coming to China. She had a home, and a friend in Yang. She was learning Chinese with surprising speed. As the Mandarin's servant she would have money week by week from the Mandarin. And with the two soldiers she could go all over the district, preaching the gospel with no danger.

As they climbed higher on the mountain trail, they passed a lovely waterfall coursing down the jagged mountain slope. The soldiers were startled as Gladys began to sing a chorus she had learned in England.

> *"What can wash away my sin?*
> *Nothing but the blood of Jesus!*
> *What can make me whole again?*
> *Nothing but the blood of Jesus!*
> *Oh, precious is the flow,*
> *That makes me white as snow-o!*
> *No other fount I know,*
> *Nothing but the blood of Jesus!"*

She stopped singing as she saw a small cluster of houses tucked into a shallow mountain valley. They were built out of the rock of the mountain and had pretty green tile roofs. A few women washing clothes in a little stream jumped up in alarm as they approached. A foreign devil with soldiers! Their tiny feet looked more like the bent hooves of goats and they were unable to run. They did their best to hobble quickly away until the soldiers called out in the name of the Mandarin, for them to halt. They must gather the village together to hear a new law. The foreign devil was the servant of the Mandarin in Yangcheng and must be obeyed.

Gladys explained that the new law forbade mothers to bind their daughters' feet. The feet of children and babies must be unbound. The woman looked mystified.

"This is impossible!" An old grandmother came toward Gladys angrily. "How will we find husbands for our daughters? No man will marry a girl with big feet!" The woman looked at Gladys's feet, small by English standards, with disgust.

"But if all the children's feet are unbound, there will *be* no tiny feet! It will not be a problem."

Now the mothers looked fearful. It would be very painful for their little girls to have to walk on unbound feet. What if they couldn't walk at all? No, the mothers couldn't bear the crying of their children.

"It is an order of the Mandarin!" Gladys said sternly. It must be done."

Seeing their distress, Gladys smiled. "I promise you, your little girls will be able to walk and run as well as the boys in your village. The pain will not last long and you will be glad never to have to bind their precious feet again. And I will help you."

Gladys crouched down beside a young mother sitting on the ground with an older woman Gladys knew the woman would be the mother-in-law. "Honourable lady, I must unbind this baby's feet," Gladys said gently to the woman. "It is the law of the Mandarin. May I begin with your granddaughter?"

The older woman gazed at the red official scroll Gladys carried, and nodded grimly. Slowly, Gladys began to unwind the strips of tight cloth around the baby's foot. Tears streamed down the mother's face.

"You must not cry," Gladys said softly. "This is a good thing for your baby. And listen; I will tell you a story as we work."

As the stained and dirty bandages came away, and the baby began to whimper in fear, Gladys began a gentle story about a man called Jesus who loved little children.

Gladys Gets a New Name

As long as the weather permitted, Gladys went on her journeys up and down the mountain to as many isolated little hamlets as she could reach. She became well known throughout the region as the wonderful "storyteller," and she made many friends. The village children went into peals of laughter at the way she acted out fairy stories for them. Gladys always changed details so that the stories became Chinese. It was a wicked warlord who poisoned Snow White's apple. Hansel and Gretel got lost in the steep paths of the Shansi Mountains and heard the lonely howling of the wolves. Robin Hood was a good bandit who stole the grain of wicked landowners and gave it to the poor of Yangcheng. But always as the villagers gathered around her at the end of their day's work, she went back to the Bible and the most wonderful stories of all. Gladys told the villagers about how God freed the Israelites. They learnt about the love of God for peasant slaves who were freed from enemies even worse than the Japanese. They saw God's great power when David the mountain shepherd became emperor of all the land. Then they heard of Jesus who was a peasant like them and who loved them and died on a bamboo cross for their sins.

Gradually some people in the villages became Christians. Little churches sprang up as villagers joined together for worship and prayer. The Bible choruses Gladys taught them rang through valleys throughout the district.

When she was in her own city of Yangcheng she was just as busy. Anything she had she would gladly give away to anyone in need. She gave help and advice to the sick. She visited the prison bringing food and medicine and telling the prisoners of Jesus who could forgive anything and who would set their hearts free.

One afternoon, as Gladys was back in Yangcheng, sweeping out the courtyard of the Inn in preparation for the mule trains that would soon be arriving, a messenger from the prison came rushing into the courtyard, almost skidding into Gladys in his haste. He bowed rapidly. "Quickly, quickly you must come! You must come! Mandarin says you must come!" He waved a red sheet of paper at Gladys, knowing she would recognize the Mandarin's official paper.

"What has happened?"

"Prisoners are killing each other. Come! Come!"

The magistrate of the prison hurried to meet Gladys as she and the messenger entered the ancient prison gate. Gladys could hear terrible shrieks coming from behind the prison walls. The prison guards were huddled in terrified groups against the outer prison walls.

"The guards will not go in," the magistrate wailed. "The prisoners have axes and they are killing each other. They will certainly kill the guards."

Gladys's heart was pounding wildly from the run to the prison. "But why have you called me? What can I do about it?" She was gasping and bowing, trying to get her breath.

"Well, you must go in and stop them!"

Gladys could taste the sudden rush of fear that swept over her. "How can *I* stop them? They will kill me, too!"

"Oh, no, they *can't!*" The magistrate nodded his head desperately. "You say you have the living God inside you. They can't kill you. You must stop them!"

Gladys felt rooted to the spot. She absolutely could not move. Nothing would make her go into the grisly battle that was raging behind the walls. She saw the soldiers watching her anxiously. She felt the magistrate's hand on her arm, urging her forward. She heard the dreadful shouts and screams and thought she could smell the blood that was pouring out in the prison yard.

"Well, was God *God* or not?" The question pounded in her mind. If He wanted her to die in that prison, die she would.

She moved forward and a few soldiers sprang to open the gate into the yard. What she saw when she entered was dreadful. Hacked and bleeding bodies lay where they fell, some of the men moaning dreadfully.

Blood was splashed everywhere and crazed men swung huge axes into anyone they could reach.

At first Gladys was not noticed. She stepped away from the wall and into the yard.

"Stop that, this instant!" she shouted. "Stop it, I tell you!" Her own fear gave force to her words. No one heard or paid attention until a prisoner with a raised machete skidded through the blood to an astonished stop a few feet away from her. He was splattered with mud and blood and his face was twisted in rage. His arm was raised to strike anyone in his path.

Her terror suddenly made her angry. " Oh no you don't, my man! Give that to me!" Gladys shot out her arm for the weapon.

The prisoner stared for a long moment as if he couldn't believe what he was seeing.

"*Give* it to me!" By now Gladys was in a rage of her own.

The man dropped the machete. Gladys picked it up, heavy as it was, and flung it behind her.

Other prisoners halted in amazement. Gladys advanced furiously into the middle of the yard. "Stop! Stop! Stop! I will help you! Stop!"

Slowly the men began to lay down their axes and machetes. The wounded prisoners cried out for help. Gladys was shaking and felt tears stinging her eyes. She thought she might fall down herself. Stamping her feet to give herself courage, she ordered the men to sit down.

"I will help you. Let someone come forward and tell me why this has happened." The prisoners were now hunched over in despair, dreading what would be in store for them.

No one moved. Finally a tall prisoner with an open slash on his arm pulled himself to his feet.

"Some prisoners have no food. There is no one to bring them anything to eat. They starve and have to watch others eating." He spoke with his eyes lowered respectfully.

"But that is not all."

"What more?" Gladys spoke gently.

"We do nothing. Some are taken away and executed but we do not know why. Some become ill but there is no doctor and they are left to suffer and die. These wounded will be left to die. We have no visitors. The wall is high. We see nothing and years pass. Sometimes it is too much and there is violence. We are ashamed and sorry."

"Tell the men to clean up the yard and bring the wounded and . . . the others . . . to the gate. Also, pile your weapons at the gate. If you do this, I will speak to the governor and the Mandarin to see what will be done about this and about the things you have told me."

The prisoner bowed. Gladys bowed. Then she walked through the gate and into the courtyard. The magistrate beamed and bowed deeply. "It is correct what I said. Your God protected you."

Gladys agreed, her voice steely. "I shall speak to the Mandarin about the conditions in this prison."

As she walked back to the Inn, the village had already heard what had happened. Some of the townsfolk who were whispering in the street bowed slightly as Gladys passed. They knew she had saved the men from terrible punishments or executions. Like her Jesus that she talked about, she had helped even despised prisoners. The convicts had given her a new name. She was no longer the small foreign devil. She was now called Ai-weh-deh, "the righteous one."

Gladys Becomes a Mother

Nowadays when Gladys went about the country, things had changed. Villagers bowed very slightly to her as she passed and were willing to stop and exchange greetings with her. Merchants no longer turned their backs on her when she passed their shops. It had been one thing to be in the Mandarin's employ as a foot inspector. Whatever she did on her long journeys into the mountains they did not know. But all by herself to stop a murderous prison riot in their own village of Yangcheng, that was heroism.

And people learned that Gladys was going to speak to the Mandarin about the prison. Gladys hoped that the Mandarin would allow the prisoners to wash themselves and their clothes in the little stream that ran just outside the prison walls. She had plans for them to obtain more food by giving them work to do. There were two old looms which the prisoners could use to make cloth. A large stone-grinding wheel had been found and soon the prisoners would be able to crush grain into flour for the noodles of Yangcheng.

How could a mere woman, even a righteous woman do such things? The women of Yangcheng viewed Gladys with awe. What they didn't know was that she viewed them with pity.

"Mandarin" she began one day when she brought her foot binding report to the Mandarin, "Is it right that husbands should be allowed to beat their wives?"

"Certainly. Wives who are disobedient to their husbands must be punished."

"But they are beaten for small things. Noodles that are not cooked properly. Taking too long to do a task. Lingering at the market. Sometimes they are badly hurt in these beatings. Does the Mandarin approve?"

"Some men can be too zealous in their punishment."

"And some men kill or sell their wives and nothing is done about it. Does the Mandarin approve?"

"We do not know that such incidents are not deserved. Perhaps the woman dishonoured her family. Perhaps she brought shame upon them."

"Mandarin, we have talked before about the love and mercy of God. It is forbidden to murder."

The Mandarin looked pleased. "It is also forbidden in China!"

"But men can kill their wives or daughters and not be punished."

"You do not understand our laws. Our laws protect the honour of men. It is men who go out from their homes to labour. Women do not need laws. They are already safeguarded in their homes by their fathers and husbands. They have only to be good daughters and good wives to live long and happy lives in their families. It has been thus for thousands of years."

"That may be!" thought Gladys as she hurried along the lane back to the Inn. "But that doesn't make it right!" As if a reminder of her unsatisfactory visit with the Mandarin, a wretched-looking woman called out to her from the other side of the path. Leaning against the woman was a thin little girl. Her hair was matted against her head and she had sores on her hands and arms. Her large black eyes were blank. Gladys thought at first the child might be blind, but she saw the child was watching her.

Gladys crossed the narrow roadway. "Woman, why are you just sitting there? Your child needs attention! The sun is beating down on her head. She is ill!"

The woman did not move. "Mind your own business, foreign devil!"

"This *is* my business!" Gladys retorted angrily. "I am the Mandarin's foot inspector. I am in charge of the welfare of children! This child looks ready to die!"

"If you care so much about her, buy her then! I will sell her for very little!" She named a small sum.

Gladys was appalled. She had known there were women who stole children and then sold them.

"What would I do with a child? And besides I have almost no money." Gladys exclaimed her eyes never leaving the gaunt little face.

"How much money *do* you have?" the woman asked.

Impulsively, Gladys thrust her hand into her jacket pocket and looked at the few coins. They totalled about nine cents in English money.

"Ninepence," Gladys answered sharply. "You wicked woman, I have ninepence."

The woman pulled herself and the child to their feet. She held out a bony hand. "She is yours!" She pushed the child away toward Gladys.

"I was so angry at her," Gladys told Yang as she introduced him to the frail new member of their household, "that I just threw the money in her hand and then she was gone. "

Yang produced a warm bowl of soup for the child who ate hungrily, scooping the noodles out of the bowl with her fingers.

"What is her name?" Yang pulled slightly away from the smell and the sight of the child and made a face.

"No idea," Gladys said cheerfully. By now she was rather enjoying herself. "Might be nice to have a child about."

"She will die soon." Yang grunted.

Gladys smiled at the child. "She is certainly *not* going to die. Her name will be Mei-en, 'Beautiful Grace' but I shall call her Ninepence."

Bombs Fall on Yangcheng

Gladys was as good as her word. Shortly after the prison riot, she asked for an audience with the Mandarin.

As usual, formalities in the beautiful palace had to be observed.

"Are you well, Mandarin?"

"I am well. Are you well?"

Gladys kept her eyes downcast in respect. "I am well, Mandarin. Are your old relatives well?"

"They are well. Are your old relatives well?"

At this question, Gladys always thought of her parents in their cosy English home. "I pray they are well, Mandarin."

"Have you eaten your food, Mandarin?"

"I have eaten my food. Have you eaten your food?"

"I have eaten my food."

Gladys gratefully took the low chair the Mandarin offered her with a slight wave of his hand.

"Mandarin, there was a riot at the prison."

The Mandarin said nothing, but Gladys knew he would have been informed.

"The prisoners are filthy and sick, and have very little food. They are chained together."

"They are criminals."

"But they are men, Mandarin. And they are treated like animals. Worse than animals."

"Why do you speak of them?"

Gladys shifted nervously in her chair. Over the years, she and the Mandarin had become friends of a sort. She had often had long conversations with him about philosophy and religion, which she knew he enjoyed. But she had never dared to criticize anything Chinese.

"If the Mandarin gave an order that the men in his prison should be allowed to wash themselves and their clothes and if they should be given food so they are not half-starved, this would bring very great honour to the Mandarin. All would know of his compassion."

"There is no honour in the washing of criminals."

"When such men are released out of the prison, they would reverence the Mandarin for his great kindness. Perhaps they would no longer steal or kill. In all of the regions in Shansi, it would be known that the Mandarin was a good and powerful ruler."

The Mandarin said nothing. Then he leaned slightly forward and looked into Gladys' eyes.

"These are difficult days, Ai-weh-deh." He used her new name with a very slight smile.

"Yes, Mandarin?"

"The Japanese army has been victorious in Manchuria. Soon they will march into China."

Gladys felt a stab of alarm.

"Will not the glorious Chinese Army stop them?"

"The dragon that attacks China has two heads. One head is Japanese. The other is Chinese. The Chinese Communists are also on the march, seeking to overthrow the National government and the Emperor. They are as cruel and bloodthirsty as the Japanese."

"All this is far away from Yangcheng, Mandarin, is it not so? Our region is remote. Surely neither the Japanese nor the Communists will travel up and down the mountain trails to reach our poor towns and villages."

A servant, deeply bowing, entered with a heavy tea tray which he lowered onto a small table at the Mandarin's side.

Gladys was glad of the distraction. She had heard rumours of fighting in the North but had given them no importance. Gratefully she accepted a round and exquisitely-decorated cup of tea from the Mandarin.

He sipped his tea thoughtfully.

"Our region is on the ancient trade routes. For hundreds, even thousands of years Shansi has been a strategic gateway to Honan and Hopeh provinces. Since the beginning of time, our mountain paths have been key trails to the East and South for traders and for armies."

Gladys spoke softly. "Then all the more reason, in dangerous times, to preach the Gospel."

"Can your God prevent the coming of the armies?"

"God is all-powerful, Mandarin. I know He is a God of peace and love. War is against His will."

"Then you must pray to your God for China." The Mandarin stood. The meeting was over. Gladys had to press her lips together to keep silent. "What about the prisoners?" She was desperate to reopen the subject. Her mind was churning in frustration and a sense of foreboding as she left the palace.

As the weeks passed, life went on as usual. Gladys also continued to enjoy her journeys as foot inspector. She was able to travel to villages several days' from Yangcheng. Everywhere she went, she saw the tiny pink toes of babies and little girls emerge from the dreadful bandages. Her beloved stories and gospel choruses echoed in the mountains. Small Christian congregations were formed.

Back in Yangcheng she continued her work at the Inn and her visits to the prison. To her delight, the Mandarin had followed her suggestions. The prisoners had more food, and they were given work to do. Under guard, they could wash themselves and their clothes in a little stream near the prison. Over time, some of the convicts became Christian believers. Life was good.

One morning while Gladys was praying in her room at the Inn, she heard the faint drone of airplanes. Reminded of the Mandarin's conversation about war, Gladys's prayers turned toward the great nation of China and its billions of people. It annoyed her that the planes seemed to be getting louder. She began to hear shouts in the street as enthralled villagers ran out to wave at the tiny silver planes that grew larger and larger in the sky.

Now the engines of the planes were suddenly roaring overhead and there were massive explosions. Gladys ran to the window. The planes were so low she could see the rising sun of the Empire of Japan on the wings of the planes. There was a deafening explosion and the floor and ceiling of her room collapsed. Gladys was flung to the courtyard of the Inn and pinned under a huge beam. Then her world went black.

Gladys is Astonished

After the bombing of Yangcheng, everything changed. The first terrible task of burying the dead was accomplished outside of the city gates. The wounded were helped as best as Gladys and her troop of surviving villagers could manage. They splinted broken bones and poured disinfectant onto wounds, bandaging them with strips of cloth ripped from towels and bedding. Men tried to clear away some of the rubble in the streets. Yang organized the cooks to prepare and distribute food so that people would not go hungry.

Everyone worked with a sense of dread and hurry. Yangcheng's position as a stop on the trade routes to the Yellow River made it an important base for the Japanese. The villagers knew that the Japanese army would be quick to enter Yangcheng, weakened as it was from the bombing. The Mandarin and his household had already gone to a safe village in the foothills. Others were with relatives in nearby villages. The people who were left needed to flee to the mountains to hide, but where?

A hastily formed committee looked to Gladys. Nobody knew the region as well as the Mandarin's foot inspector. Where did she advise them to go?

"I know of a Christian village, a day's journey from Yangcheng, that would be a safe place. They will take us in." Gladys spoke as cheerfully and decisively as she could. Her real feelings were far from optimistic. Who could tell what Japanese they might meet on the way? "The Japanese may come at any moment. We must leave today."

The straggle of villagers looked doubtful. There were so many wounded and sick. Everyone was exhausted. "As soon as possible!" There was a slightly desperate tone in Gladys's raised voice. "Today!"

The people gathered together what food and little comforts they could carry and, led by a very tired Gladys, a little group of about forty shell-shocked souls trudged out of their beloved and ruined Yangcheng toward the tiny mountain hamlet of Bei Chai Chuang. Some of the wounded were carried in makeshift litters. Mothers tucked babies in baskets balanced at the ends of long poles across their shoulders. The tiny steps of so many small children slowed their march and the groans of the wounded were agonizing to hear.

At long last they reached Bei Chai Chuang. There were Christians throughout the region and in Bei Chai Chung. Here they were welcomed and helped. Gladys was greatly relieved to see her little group safely in one place, for the time being at least. She knew that as the days went by some would creep back to Yangcheng in hopes that the Japanese would have come and gone. Others would seek out distant relatives who lived beyond the ancient mule paths that the Japanese army used. The Japanese knew nothing of the secret paths up and down the mountains that the village people used.

Gladys knew them all. And she well understood the dire struggle of the Chinese army against the Japanese and the Communists. But as the winter of 1939 passed into spring and then into summer, Gladys knew nothing of the storms of war that were gathering in far-off Europe. The historic third day of September 1939, was a day like any other to Gladys. She knew nothing of the dreadful headlines filling the papers back in London: in response to German and Japanese aggression, Britain had declared war on both countries. If she had known, Gladys might have said she had quite enough to think about with the Japanese invading China! She might have worried for a moment about her family in England, but then, German planes would never be able to reach England!

What Gladys had most to be concerned about was a new and dreadful thing happening in the mountain villages and fields throughout Shansi. The Chinese army had ordered a "scorched earth" policy for the province. That meant that in the regions in which the Japanese were advancing all crops and villages were to be burnt so that nothing would be left for the Japanese troops. No food. No shelter.

In the midst of her dismay, the Mandarin sent a message to Gladys that he wanted to see her.

"But Mandarin!" Gladys cried when she reached the Mandarin. "Nothing will be left for us *Chinese*. What will the people do?"

The Mandarin smiled at Gladys now calling herself Chinese. He knew she had become a Chinese citizen. He had heard the story of how Ai-weh-deh had burned her British passport. There was a sigh behind his smile. That British passport might have saved her if she were caught by the Japanese.

"People must hide in the mountains. In caves or small villages. They must find little places where they can grow grain. They must also kill Japanese wherever they find them."

Gladys felt sick. She had already seen enough of dead bodies. But perhaps such killing would never happen. "How will they kill Japanese? They have no guns."

"They will take guns from dead Japanese. Our glorious Army of China is fighting valiantly, pushing back the Japanese army when they can find them. We have already lost Manchuria. We are determined to lose not one meter more of China to the wicked Empire of Japan!"

"I remember the fighting in Manchuria, Mandarin. I tried to come all the way to China on the train, but the war prevented it."

The Mandarin gazed at Gladys for a long moment. "Your God brought you to China through great danger. And now you are in great danger again. It seems your fate to live in perilous times."

Gladys was a little surprised that the Mandarin mentioned "her" God. She had had many conversations with the Mandarin about religion. He had asked interesting questions, but had never accepted that "her" God was real and that He acted in the lives of mere mortals and most certainly not in the life of his most lowly foot inspector!

"Our old ways in Shansi are now gone," he continued. "I wish to give a last feast in Yangcheng. At the feast I will make an announcement. Many have returned to Yangcheng and are trying to make a life again. The Mandarin will not return. This will be a last meeting with the village officials. You also must attend."

Gladys wore her one festive satin dress to the feast. It was yellow silk and embroidered with green ferns and flowers. She loved its great wide sleeves and stand-up collar to which she had pinned a pretty broach. As usual at such events, she was the only woman present. This time she was given the place of honour next to the Mandarin. Attending were the governor of the prison, the formerly wealthy merchants and village officials. In spite of the bad times, the lanterns the Mandarin had ordered strung around the room gave off a rosy glow. Even the food, simple as it now had to be, was the nicest she had tasted in months.

After the meal, the Mandarin rose to speak. To her surprise, he began to tell the story of how Gladys had come to China, and of her many adventures and exploits: her work at the Inn and how the muleteers all learned that it was the best Inn in Yangcheng. How she quickly learned the Chinese language so that she spoke perfect Shansi dialect. How she had been an excellent foot inspector and how she had helped people everywhere she went, giving anything she had to ease the lives of the peasants. She had adopted a Chinese child as her own and she had become a Chinese citizen. And always when she was asked why she came to China, she answered in the same way.

The Mandarin looked down at Gladys, whose face was flushed with embarrassment.

"She always answers that she came to tell about Jesus, about his love for us Chinese and his forgiveness of sin and his salvation. She says no one could have cared more for us Chinese and for China than Jesus. For many years I felt that it was only Ai-weh-deh herself who cared for China."

Gladys didn't want to appear to disagree in public with the Mandarin, but anyone watching her and hearing the Mandarin's last sentence would have noticed a slight shake of her head in disagreement. "It is *Jesus* who cares!" she was longing to say.

The Mandarin's next sentence utterly amazed her.

"And now I say to Ai-weh-deh, I wish to follow this Jesus who loves China; I wish to become a Christian!"

Tears of astonished joy filled Gladys's eyes.

Gladys Becomes a Spy

In spite of her happiness at the conversion of her old friend the Mandarin, Gladys's heart was heavy at the suffering she saw around her. People were hungry. Many had lost their homes and loved ones and were living in mountain caves with only small night fires to keep them from freezing. The villagers told terrible stories about the cruelty of the Japanese soldiers. They knew they would receive no mercy if the Japanese found them.

Gladys had returned to the mission station at Tsechow where she had first found refuge in her early days in China. The little group of missionaries in the compound tried to insist that they were on ground consecrated to God. No soldiers could be admitted – not Chinese soldiers, not Japanese, and not Communist.

From the relative safety of the mission she continued to visit the little villages and Christian communities in the cold Shansi Mountains. These hamlets were so remote that often the people knew very little about the war. They carried on their simple lives as their ancestors had been doing for hundreds of years. When Gladys arrived, there would be hymn singing, Bible reading and prayer meetings. Often Gladys was refreshed and cheered to be away from more populated areas where people lived with the fear that at any moment they might have to flee from the Japanese.

When Gladys travelled into Japanese controlled territory she did her best to evade notice, taking roundabout paths and hunching over her mule if she suddenly encountered a party of Japanese soldiers. What did they care about a little Chinese woman all by herself riding on a mule in the mountains?

The winter had been very hard but all of Shansi dreaded the Spring. As little green shoots began pressing up from the hard earth and the fluttering of birds began to be seen, fear grew. Spring would bring the marching of armies as the trade routes in the mountains again become passable.

"Keep those soldiers out of here!" Gladys called early one morning at the mission in Tsechow. She had noticed four Chinese soldiers peering in at the mission gate. One of the Bible women at the mission looked uncertain.

"But they are Chinese *Nationalist* soldiers!" she called. Surely it would be all right to let in noble soldiers of the Chinese army!

Gladys sped to the courtyard, her temper rising.

"You cannot come in here!" She exclaimed, half-running to the gate. "This is a Christian *mission!* We have nothing to do with the fighting and soldiers!"

She stopped in front of a tall officer, glaring up at him as he bowed to her.

"You are the honourable Ai-weh-deh?"

"I am, but you still can't come in here." Gladys was surprised at his beautiful manners.

"We have come from Generalissimo Chiang Kai-shek. We seek your help."

Gladys was seldom at a loss for words but for the moment she was utterly silent. General Chiang Kai-shek? The great hero? The President of China?

"I am Colonel Linnan. The Generalissimo told us to seek out Christians if we needed shelter. He and Madame Chiang-Kei-shek are Christian believers and they have great trust in Christians. I am very sorry to have troubled you." The Colonel bowed deeply.

Gladys continued to stare. The officer was tall with clear olive skin and gentle black eyes. His uniform was spotless, his boots polished to a high shine. He spoke in the beautiful Mandarin of a highly educated person. She could believe that he represented the President.

Finally she found her voice and her Chinese manners. She bowed. "Forgive me for my words. We at this mission must be very careful to remain outside of the fighting. "

Colonel Linnan gave her a slight nod which seemed to say, "I understand but I do not necessarily agree."

"If your esteemed companions would leave, we would be honoured if you would accept refreshment from our humble household."

On the Colonel's orders the three soldiers accompanying him turned toward the street and were gone.

Then over streaming cups of pale tea, Colonel Linnan told Gladys that he was a member of the Chinese intelligence service. It was his responsibility to send information back to headquarters where military plans and decisions were made.

"Shansi province is an area vital to the defence of China," he explained. "It is the gateway south to the Yellow River. It is of utmost importance that we defeat the Japanese army here in this province to stop their advance further into China. But the situation here is very confused."

"Yes." Gladys poured more tea into the Colonel's small cup. "We know very well how important this area is to the Japanese. We have been bombed. Our villages have been burned to the ground and many people killed. After a bombing, the Japanese army advances; there is terrible fighting and then they are driven back by our army. Then they return. We never know which army is succeeding."

"Exactly. But these mountainous regions can be defended easily if only we knew the location of the Japanese forces and what route through the mountains they were taking."

"I see them very often on my travels," Gladys remarked. "I never know where they will be myself."

"On your travels?" Linnan was startled. "Surely you do not travel in these times. And by yourself?"

"Certainly I do!" Gladys drew her small frame straight up in her chair. "I came to China to preach the gospel, and no Japanese army is going to stop me! I go all over the mountains even behind the Japanese lines. The Japanese don't bother me. What do they want with me? I am just a woman on a mule."

Linnan had a quiet dignity that reminded Gladys of the Mandarin in Yangcheng. "You could help China, if you are willing," he said quietly.

"I love China!" Gladys felt a bit cross although she did not show it. Did he think she didn't love China? "I am a Chinese citizen," she added. "Changed my citizenship from British to Chinese ages ago."

The smile Linnan gave to Gladys was beautiful. It seemed a long time since anyone had smiled at her or had spoken so gently to her. "I understand that as a Christian worker, you wish to be neutral so that in keeping Chinese soldiers away, you might be able to keep away the Japanese."

Gladys nodded.

"But you are a Chinese citizen and a Christian. Is it not your sacred duty to help your people? Many Chinese lives might be saved with the information you could give us about the locations of the Japanese forces. It is not only Chinese soldiers who would be saved, but the people of the countryside too."

Gladys thought of the terrible suffering that had come upon Shansi province at the hands of the Japanese. They spared no one and they especially hated Christians who were more concerned about obeying their God than Japanese soldiers!

"Who would I tell? I cannot be seen speaking with Chinese soldiers."

Colonel Linnan smiled his smile again. "I am stationed here in Tsechung. I will visit the mission every week or so, after dark of course. You will not be seen speaking to me."

Well, God had made Gladys an innkeeper in China. A foot inspector. A mother and a nurse. If He wanted her to be a spy, so be it!

"I will help you if I can, for the sake of dear China."

Linnan stood up and bowed. "May your God greatly reward you. I will return for 'tea' in a week."

Gladys Falls in Love

Linnan was as good as his word. In one week, as he had promised, after the little group at the Mission had finished their evening meal and prayers, there was a soft knock on the door. The gate to the compound was always shut at dusk, but Gladys had given the gatekeeper instructions to open it for Linnan.

She hurried him into a small room lit by a rosy lantern. "We can talk here."

Linnan bowed. His eyes searched her face. "Are you well?"

For some reason Gladys blushed. What was the matter with her? His question was the correct way to begin a conversation among cultured Chinese. Still there was something about the way he asked it that had made her blush.

"I am well. Are you well?"

Linnan nodded without answering as if he wanted to do away with the formal courtesies.

"You have been on a journey?"

"Yes. I was two days' journey from Tsechow. I visited Chin Shui."

"Are you not afraid of bandits? These missionary travels are dangerous. Something could happen in the mountains and there would be no one to help you."

Gladys laughed. "But I am now an informant! How else can I get information for you but by travelling? Surely you don't worry about the safety of your spies!"

Linnan's dark eyes revealed nothing but his voice was soft. "I'm afraid I do worry about you!"

Gladys blushed again. She became so flustered she frowned. "Well, you don't need to!" Her words were sharper than she intended. She smoothed the silk of her gown. Why had she put on her best gown? She was becoming a silly creature. She composed herself.

"I did see some Japanese soldiers near Chin Shui. They were perhaps half a day's journey from the village."

"How many?" Linnan leaned forward in his chair and took out a small notebook.

"I saw, perhaps, twenty. They were taking food from a small village market. They took almost all the food. More, I think than what twenty soldiers would need. The poor peasants could do nothing to stop them. They were terrified."

"Officers?"

"I don't think so. I stayed on the edges of the market. I am not keen to come to the notice of a Japanese soldier!"

"Quite right! That's right. I want you to take great care! You must be as safe as possible at all times, Ai-weh-deh. You must do nothing to put yourself in danger."

Never before in China had anyone cared about *her* welfare! *She* was the one who took care of everyone else. Was this something Linnan said to all his informants?

"Oh, I'll be all right!" Gladys shrugged. "Nobody worries about *me*!"

"Please pardon me, Ai-weh-deh, but you are quite wrong. I worry about you alone on the mountains!"

It was lovely to have someone concerned about her! Gladys knew she was feeling pleased.

"Let us have tea," she suggested. "I want to know how you came to be a Colonel in the Chinese army and what you think about in your long journeys across China."

In the weeks that followed, Gladys and Linnan worked out a kind of schedule for her travels and their visits. She became better and better at gathering information as she went about in the mountains. When she saw no Japanese, often the villagers would tell her where they were or how recently they had seen them. When she came across a camp of Japanese soldiers, instead of ignoring them, she slowed her mule and made him walk as if he were so old he was about to die on the spot. As her mule plodded past she counted their numbers while giving them sideways glances.

As soon as she was out of sight, she smacked her mule smartly on its side. She was impatient to get back to Tsechow. The information meetings with Linnan had turned into night walks along the river where they also talked about China, its immense history and philosophy, the beauty of its landscape and what they might do after the war.

Gladys had never been so happy in her life. Others noticed how easily she laughed, how promptly she returned from her missionary journeys. "We can set a clock by Gladys, these days!" One of the Bible teachers at the mission grinned mischievously. "It used to be we never knew when she would turn up, but these days, she is very prompt in giving her reports to Colonel Linnan!"

One day, one of the senior missionaries, a kindly British preacher called David Davis came to Gladys. "You have been working so hard, Gladys, we want to give you a rest for a few days!

Gladys looked sceptical.

"No, Gladys, you will enjoy it! At Lingchuang there is a small missions conference next week and you ought to go. It will be a bit of a holiday for you and you deserve it. We have already made arrangements and the Christians there are so pleased that you will be coming."

Gladys first thought was that she would miss her weekly meeting with Linnan! She was surprised by the power of dismay she felt. If she hadn't realized it before, in that moment she realized that her friendship with Linnan had deepened into love. This would not do! She must not centre her life on personal feelings! She was a missionary!

"Well, if you think I should go..."

"We certainly think so! It will be good for you, Gladys. You need a rest."

"No! I really need to see Linnan!" she thought. But her smile did not betray her feelings. "I can't remember when I've been to a conference. I know I will enjoy it."

What Gladys didn't know was that it would be a very long time before she would see Linnan again.

Gladys Becomes a Fugitive

It was not far to the missionary conference at Lingchuang, only a journey of four hours or so. Gladys was travelling with three Bible workers, Chung-Ru-mai, Timothy and Sualan from the mission compound. As they neared the town, Gladys was telling the story of how she came to adopt several children. The workers knew about Ninepence. But how had the little boy, Les, come to her?

"I was cooking our midday meal at our Inn in Yangcheng. Ninepence had been playing with some children along the road so I had to call her to come for her meal. 'Mother,' she said, 'there is a boy outside our gate who has nowhere to go. He has no mother or father.'

"It was already the time when food was getting scarce and expensive so I told her we did not have money to buy extra food. I thought that would end the discussion but Ninepence then said, 'Mother, if I ate a little less, and you ate a little less, wouldn't there be food for him?' "

Gladys made a silly face and they all laughed. "What could I say? We called him 'Les' after Ninepence's pleading. And one by one other children came."

There was a faint buzz in the air. Gladys pulled her mule to a stop and scanned the sky. Tiny silver specs could be seen on the horizon. Everyone now recognized the hum of Japanese planes, the flashes in the sunlit sky that rained death. "Quickly! Away from the road!" Gladys swung off her mule and people fled in all directions into the fields. The donkeys brayed in terror at the pandemonium as they were dragged and pushed into a thicket of sparse shrubbery growing in a nearby field. Gladys' little group flung themselves as far into the bushes as they could, covering their ears against one deafening explosion after another as the Japanese bombs fell on Lingchuang.

Only too well could Gladys picture what was happening inside the city walls. Bodies falling, children's screams, blood. Buildings collapsing or bursting into flames. People running in every direction. A thick haze of smoke and dust. The roar of plane engines. The moaning of the wounded as the planes circled away.

When it was quiet again, they mounted their mules and were soon in the city. The damage was not as terrible as it had been at Yangcheng. People now knew what the hum of planes meant and they would flee into the hills at the first sight or sound of an aeroplane. But still, the day was long as the little conference tried to meet for a few hours in prayer and Bible reading.

That night, Gladys could not sleep. She was exhausted but awake with a sense of deep foreboding. "We must get out of the city! We must be the first out of the city when the city gates open!" The thought was so persistent that she woke her three companions.

"Get up" she whispered. They were perched, according to custom, on the long brick stove platform, wedged in among many other sleepers.

"It's still night!" Timothy groaned in protest.

"We must be first out the gate. Get up! Sualan and Chung-Ru-Mai, wake up!"

In the commotion of the whispers and movement, others woke up. It was still three hours before the gates would open but if Ai-weh-deh was leaving, they were leaving too!

Huddled against the huge city gate in the cold night air, no one looked cheerful. Gladys felt both foolish and anxious. She watched the full moon slowly descend behind the distant mountains. At long last the sky began to lighten. She saw crowds of city-dwellers pressing toward the gate, their numbers reaching far back into the town. They knew that after bombings, the Japanese came. The town leaders would then be killed and many others who angered the Japanese for one reason or another, or for no reason at all.

The gatekeeper's progress through the crowds was slow. He was pushing his way through, muttering and shaking his head, his huge keys jangling on their ring as he trudged along. Finally he reached the gate. With a great clatter he slammed back the huge bolts and unlocked the ancient wooden gates.

"Come on!" Gladys snatched up her bundles and shoved her little group through the gates. Once they were outside the walls and walking quickly away, Gladys glanced behind. A stream of refugees was winding slowly out of the city. Gladys smiled to herself at the foolish thought that she was like the Pied Piper leading the children out of Hamelin. Or Moses leading the children of Israel!

It was a lovely morning of sunshine and birdsong. Dawn streaked the sky with pink and gold. But coming over the horizon she saw two groups of cavalry, the soldiers riding their horses hard. W*hose* soldiers? With relief she made out the uniforms of the Chinese army. The refugees stopped walking to watch them come. They bowed in respect as the horses pounded past. It was unusual for the army not to wave at villagers as they passed. Their faces were grim.

Then came a familiar faint hum, getting louder. In a flash, Gladys knew what was about to happen. The Japanese planes were targeting the soldiers. This time there would not be bombing. There would be a terrible storm of machine gun fire, the planes circling again and again until nothing moved. The carnage would be unspeakable.

"Run to the fields!" Gladys screamed to the crowd. "Run! And then get down! Run! Run!"

The long winding line suddenly broke as the crowd realized what was about to happen. People fled in all directions into the fields. Throwing themselves flat they pressed into the ground. The soldiers, still galloping wildly to reach the protection of the city, had no chance. Neither did the crowds of people still pouring out of the city gates.

Nothing Gladys had seen at Yancheng and other bombed villages had prepared her for the dreadful scene after the planes left. There was a young doctor among the survivors and Gladys and the doctor worked through the terrible hours of the day doing what they could for the wounded. Everyone who was able staggered away from Lingchuang to the caves in the mountains. Only there could they hope to escape the Japanese offensive. All of the towns in the regions would be attacked as the Japanese advanced.

Gladys joined the villagers in the caves. For the next six weeks they lived in the cold caves, eating bits of grain boiled in water that people had carried with them. Boys crept out into the countryside to search for any little hamlet in an effort to buy any food they could. Starving wolves patrolled outside of the cave, their unearthly howling waking children in the night. Never had Gladys felt so alone.

Little did she know that there was one person who was looking everywhere for her.

Gladys Makes a Decision

Colonel Linnan had been searching for Gladys for three whole weeks. He knew she had set off to attend a conference in Lingchuang and that the city had been heavily bombed. She would have no way of knowing that in spite of the Japanese attacks, the Chinese army had been successful in driving back the Japanese. If she were hiding, he had to find her!

Two days after the bombing of Lingchuang he had ordered his soldiers to look for any signs of her in every ruined street and building. He himself spent countless hours moving rubble, crawling over the heaps of debris from collapsed houses, dreading what he might find at any moment. Others of his soldiers questioned all the villagers. "Had a foreign lady been buried?" Others carefully searched the fields around the city. They found many bodies but they did not find Gladys.

"Colonel Linnan," one of his men bowed respectfully. "Is this anything? I found it in the grain field a short way beyond the city gate." He held out a small book.

Linnan took the book. It was a Christian hymnbook. On the front page was Gladys' name in Chinese characters. "This is Ai-weh-deh's hymn book. It means she escaped the city!" he exclaimed in relief. "Call the men! She may be hiding in a cave near the city! They must search the caves around Lingchang! That's where we will find her."

But his high hopes had not been realized. High in the mountain cave, things were not going well for the little group of refugees. Weeks of cold and little food had made them all half-sick and very discouraged. Gladys's newest little son, Timothy, was looking paler and thinner every day. Increasingly, Gladys was becoming concerned that farmers in the area were now aware of them. Their urgent trips into the tiny villages were becoming known. "Who could know who might betray them to the Japanese?"

"We must move on," she would say. "We are in danger of some informant telling the Japanese we are hiding here. If they find us hiding, they will shoot us."

The group was irritable and exhausted. They refused. They were tired and full of fear. "We might meet the Japanese in these mountains if we leave."

"Where can we go? We can't return to Lingchuang. It is destroyed."

"No village will allow us to stay with them. We are strangers and if the Japanese find us, the whole village will be punished."

"We will only have to find another cave. It's just as well we stay in this one!"

Days passed and still Gladys felt a strong urging to leave. Was God telling her they must move on? Finally she could stand it no longer.

"I am leaving this minute! I will take Timothy with me and go to the end of the valley. If there is danger, we will come back and tell you. In a few days you must set out and join us."

"If the Japanese kill you, there will be no one to tell us that!"

Gladys smiled. "Don't you think God can protect me against the Japanese?"

The group was silent. "Possibly," they seemed to be thinking. "But some Christians *have* been killed by the Japanese. Japanese hate Christians because they do not always obey their cruel orders."

"Timothy and I will be very careful. If there are Japanese nearby, we will certainly see them before they see us. We will simply hide where we are until dark, and then return to you."

Without waiting for new arguments, Gladys began gathering her few possessions in a bundle. What a shame she had lost her hymnbook in the flight from Lingchuang. Still, she had her Bible.

The journey down the mountain and along the valley floor would have been almost pleasant if it hadn't been for their hunger and the worry Gladys felt about coming upon the Japanese. Timothy was delighted to be free from the confines of the cave. He ran along ahead of Gladys, stopping to examine a pretty wild flower now and then or to look for a bird whose song he could hear from some distant bush.

As they climbed up a rather steep hill along the path, they paused at the top to rest. Gladys' heart jumped at what she saw. In the distance there was a line of soldiers on horseback advancing slowly, obviously searching for people who might be hiding.

"Timothy, run back to the cave and tell everybody to go up the mountain as far as they can. There are soldiers."

Obedient little Timothy was gone in a flash.

Gladys walked as boldly as she could in the direction of the soldiers. When she was close enough to shout, she yelled, "Here I am if you are looking for me!"

The officer leading the group suddenly began to gallop toward her. Gladys stood still, screwing up her eyes and praying, "God help me! God help me! God help me!"

The pounding hooves stopped beside her. Then a voice said, "Ai-weh-deh, my dear! I have been looking everywhere for you!"

It was Linnan. How wonderful it was to see him! His happiness about having found her, and having found her alive and well, touched her deeply. Together with Timothy they returned to the cave just in time to stop the little group from leaving to join Gladys. Eagerly they gathered around Linnan as he told them the news.

It would be better for them to stay in the cave he told them. The Japanese were fighting ferociously for Tsechow. When it was safe to return there, he would send a messenger. He would also send food to their cave from time to time.

After a simple meal, Gladys and Linnan left the cave for a quiet spot where they could be alone to talk.

"Gladys, when it is possible, I want to send soldiers to take you to safety across the Yellow River to free China. You are not safe here."

Gladys thought for a moment before she replied. How lovely it would be to be away from the bombing, the constant hunger and all the suffering. She took a deep breath. "Of course I cannot go."

Linnan took her hand. "You *must* go! I cannot be always worried about you; where you are, if you are all right. Searching for you if I don't know where you are. My mind must be on fighting this war."

"You don't *need* to worry about me! God takes care of me!"

Linnan looked grave. "We have thought, have we not, Ai-weh-deh, of perhaps, marriage someday?"

A warmth spread over Gladys. She looked down in her smile. "Someday, perhaps."

"Then as your future husband, you must obey me. You have no father here to counsel you!"

Gladys bristled a little. "I have my heavenly Father!"

Linnan shook his head. "Gladys, you *must* allow me to send you to safety. I cannot always be worrying about you, not knowing if you are dead or alive. There can be no question of you staying in Shansi. "

Gladys took her hand from Linnan's and walked a few steps away. She could hardly bear to say the words.

"Linnan, we must part."

"Yes, I know," he said. "Soon enough, I will be sent somewhere else. That's just the reason…"

Gladys interrupted. "You are a soldier and an officer and it is a time of war. All your energies must go to fighting the Japanese. I understand this. And you must understand that I will never leave my people. You must not try to get me out of this."

"I think you must obey me," Linnan said quietly.

Gladys searched for the words that would change their lives. Slowly she said, "Linnan we must part. I must obey God and be a missionary. You must obey your superiors and be a soldier. It is impossible for us to have a life together. I should have known. We must say goodbye." Gladys' voice was full of tears.

Linnan stood a very long time gazing at Gladys. The mountain was so still she could hear a breeze rustling the leaves of little bushes. High in the sky she saw a bird swooping toward the earth. Finally, without a word, Linnan bowed deeply and left.

In a few moments, she heard the pounding of his horse as he galloped down the mountain. Gladys knew she would never see him again.

Gladys Begins Her Epic Journey

For three anxious years Gladys, the small band of children she adopted, and many other refugees were on the front line of the fighting. Yangcheng, the lovely hamlet where she and Mrs. Lawson had started their Inn, was the centre of the fighting. Four times it had changed hands. First, the Chinese army defended it, then after intense fighting, the Japanese would occupy the city. There would be more intense fighting and then the Chinese army would succeed in driving the Japanese out.

When the battle in the region was intense, people would flee to the caves and live on whatever little food they could carry. Often they ate young weeds that grew in the rocky mountain soil. They would stay in the caves for days or weeks, depending on how close the combat raged.

When there was a pause in the fighting, Gladys returned to the mission in Tsechow. From here she would swing her small body onto a mule and make her familiar way throughout the mountain villages, preaching, holding prayer meetings, visiting friends and giving all the information and practical help she could. She trained countrywomen in first aid and tried to link them with the Red Cross. She held the hands of frightened young mothers who were in labour. She washed and bandaged the wounded, comforted the grieving, told stories everywhere. Often on her return, there would be a tiny orphan in her arms or small orphan children walking beside her mule.

Also on her return she would find an officer friend or two in the Chinese Nationalist Army to report what she had seen and what local villagers had told her. Gladys didn't like to think of herself as a *spy*. She was a Chinese citizen doing what she could to help her country.

One morning after prayers, David came to her with a worry line across his forehead. "Gladys, I very much need to talk to you." He waved to the wicker chairs on the mission house veranda. He looked so serious that Gladys sat without an argument, although after morning prayers she always hurried to her room for her own quiet time with God.

"David, what has happened?"

"Gladys, you know the Japanese are very suspicious of Western foreigners and especially foreign missionaries. Missionaries will not bow to Hirohito, the divine Emperor of Japan. We have reports of British missionaries being killed."

"I am not British. I am a Chinese citizen!"

"I doubt very much if that will help you."

"*Help* me?"

"Someone has betrayed you to the Japanese. They know you are a spy. They have put a price on your head. Look, here is a leaflet offering the reward."

Gladys took the small paper David held out and examined it carefully. Sure enough there was her name. It read, "Any person giving information which leads to the capture, alive or dead of Ai-weh-deh, will receive a reward of one hundred pounds from the Japanese High Command." She handed the leaflet back to David.

David put the paper down on a nearby table. "The Japanese are sure that the information about where they are camped in the mountains is coming from you."

"As it certainly is!" Gladys looked a bit satisfied. "Good for them that they know Chinese citizens will help our country."

"Gladys. The reward for your capture is one hundred pounds!"

Gladys snorted in disbelief. "What nonsense! One hundred pounds for *me*? What utter foolishness!"

David Davies sighed impatiently. "You are in the greatest danger. You must take this seriously! The Japanese are expected to invade Tsechow and Yangcheng any minute. Even today or tomorrow!"

"Well, I'm not going to run away! God brought me here and God will take care of me. The silliness of the Japanese! One hundred pounds!"

David tried another argument. "You are putting all the children here in danger. If the Japanese come for you, they will find the children. The older boys they will steal and force them to fight for Japan. The girls they will steal for their evil purposes. The little ones they will shoot."

Gladys pressed her hands against her chest and took a slow deep breath. "David, this reward changes nothing! We are always in danger. But I *cannot* go and leave our people. There is the preaching and the Bible studies and caring for the wounded and sick. The people need me more than ever and especially now if the Japanese are coming. How can I possibly leave them? And we can hide if the Japanese come!"

David shook his head. "We do hope and pray for God's protection of course. But the Japanese are sure to find you if you stay here, Gladys. Everyone knows Ai-weh-deh. A hundred pounds is a fortune in these days. Someone will lead them to you. What terrible things the Japanese do to spies and women prisoners, we must not think about."

Gladys suddenly felt a little sick.

"Where could I go?"

"You must get to Sian and cross the Yellow River to unoccupied China. The cities on the other side of the river are teeming with refugees and orphans. There will be much for you to do there."

"How can I run away to safety and leave my people here to face the Japanese? I can't do it! You are in as much danger as I am, David, and you are staying, aren't you?"

"I'm not a spy, Gladys," David answered gently. "I do not have a price on my head."

"How can I leave all the children? And my own children in Yangcheng?" Gladys knew that at that moment three of her adopted children were in school learning to write Chinese. Her precious Ninepence was helping in the mission at her old Inn.

"I will make arrangements for the children here. And when the Japanese have been driven out of Shansi, you will come back."

"Never, never, never will I leave!" Gladys felt completely determined. "This is where God called me to be and I will live or die here, it's up to him."

David shook his head helplessly. He had been afraid Gladys would be stubborn

"It's my prayer time." Gladys picked up her Bible from a nearby table and stood resolutely. "I will pray about all this David, but you can be sure that I am not leaving."

Gladys Has a Problem

Gladys knelt by her narrow bed and poured out her heart to the Lord. "Lord, You know I cannot leave the children and the dear people here in Tsechow. You know you have called me to minister in this place and I am willing to stay here and die here if that is your will. Please protect us all from the Japanese. Let there be no more bombing and killing in this place. Guide us and shelter us under your wings."

On and on she prayed, and the tumult in her heart gradually quieted. A peaceful confidence came over her. The Lord would guide and shelter! Finally, getting up from her knees, she sat on her bed and opened her Chinese Bible. She stared in amazement hardly daring to breathe. The word, "Flee!" was the first word she saw. "Flee ye; flee ye into the mountains; dwell deeply in hidden places, because the king of Babylon has conceived a purpose against you." Over and over she read the words, "Flee. Flee ye to the mountains!"

All her Christian life Gladys had had no trouble immediately obeying the Lord when she knew the Lord was speaking to her. Today was no exception although she was very surprised that the Lord was telling her to leave. She thought quickly: David would send the Tsechow children in small groups of three or four over the mountains with Christian leaders. That would be all right. The Japanese would not be looking for a "father" travelling with his children. But what of the children in Yangcheng and her own children there? There was no one who could take them into the mountains. The older Bible women who were caring for the orphans were too frail. The able-bodied men were in the army or had been killed. She would have to get to Yangcheng, Japanese army or no Japanese army, gather up the children there and flee as the Lord commanded.

The Bible women in Yangcheng stared at Gladys in amazement. How had she come? The whole of Shansi Province was now occupied by the Japanese. The Japanese were looking everywhere for her. The women glanced nervously at the door as if they expected Japanese soldiers to burst in at any moment and arrest Gladys.

Gladys had no time for chatting. "You must get the children ready. We will leave at first light tomorrow. I'm taking them to free China where they will be safe and cared for."

The women stared at Gladys. "Which children would she take? Who would go with her?"

"Well, all of them, of course!" Gladys was tired from her journey from Tsechow. Once she had been spotted by some Japanese soldiers who chased her and shot at her. Finally the soldiers had given up as she raced higher and higher up the mountain slopes. She needed to rest and have something to eat.

"*All* of them? There are almost one hundred children here."

Now Gladys began feeling cross. "There is no one else to take them. They will have to come with me."

The oldest of the Bible women stepped toward Gladys and gave her a sisterly bow. "Dear sister, dear Ai-weh-deh, this is impossible. There is no food for the children in the mountains. And how can you evade the Japanese if you have one hundred children with you? And where will they sleep? And how can small children walk to the Yellow River?"

"Nothing is impossible with God. God will have to provide for us, that's all." Gladys fixed them with a stern look. "Have the children ready to leave in the morning. They must carry a cup and bowl and a little lunch. They should wear the warmest clothes they have. Those who can, should carry a blanket and extra food."

Gladys saw that the deep orange late afternoon sun was sinking below the mountains. "I must sleep now," she said. "As early as possible tomorrow we begin our journey."

The small children were thrilled! A picnic in the mountains. No school. An adventure.

The older children packed baskets with as much food as they could carry. Gladys saw they were fearful. Yes, God would be with them, but the mountains and roads were filled with Japanese soldiers. And how could they live for weeks on the mountains? Still, Ai-weh-deh would be with them.

Marching out of the city gates the children skipped along, energized by the unaccustomed freedom. For such a long time they had been confined to the safety of their village. Now the whole world was open to them! Ninepence and the rest of Gladys's children walked with her, helping in many small ways with the little ones.

Someone's shoe had come off. Someone's cup had been lost, the child wailing as the cup rolled down a steep mountain path. Someone begged to be carried. Someone was bitten by a bug. Someone thought a Japanese soldier had been sighted.

The long days passed slowly. When they came to remote mountain villages, they were able to buy food. Sometimes they slept in sheds; sometimes they slept with the goats to keep warm. Even in the high places they might come across a Buddhist temple where the priest would give them permission to shelter for the night. They would huddle together on the polished floor, hoping to keep the rats away, glad of a roof to keep out the midnight cold. Once they came upon an encampment of Chinese soldiers. The soldiers welcomed the children to their campfires and gave them sweets and an evening meal. The children stuffed themselves with as much food as they could eat and for the first time in as far as most of them could remember, they were not hungry when they fell asleep.

Into the second week, their progress was slow. The small children had to be carried. The older children often limped from blisters on their swollen feet. Their cloth shoes were in tatters. They had to stop for rest much more often. Sometimes Gladys carried two of the little ones in her arms at the same time. Another child might be clutching her skirt, dragged along by Gladys' steps.

On the twelfth day as they came to the top of one of the foothills, glittering in the distance, they could see the far-off ribbon of light that was the Yellow River. The children were too tired to be excited but smiles of relief lit their faces. Soon they would be safe from the Japanese. They would have food. They would have new shoes once their swollen and blistered feet healed. They would sleep indoors and be warm! Gladys rallied them as they stumbled their way to the river.

"Come on, children!" she called. "We are almost there! Let's sing!" Their familiar gospel chorus rang through the mountains:

"When upon life's billows you are tempest-tossed,
When you are discouraged thinking all is lost,
Count your many blessings, name them one by one
And it will surprise you what the Lord has done.

> *Count your blessings,*
> *Name them one by one*
> *Count your blessings,*
> *See what God hath done*
> *Count your blessings,*

> *Name them one by one,*
> *Count your many blessings*
> *See what God hath done."*

The Yellow River! Free China! Gladys felt almost light-headed with relief! No more fear of the Japanese! And on the banks of the Yellow River they would find the village of Yuan Chu. The Japanese army couldn't have come so far. There would be food for the children. Villagers would help them! With their last reserves of energy, the straggling, staggering band of children wove their way down the foothills, Gladys leading the way.

Two of the older boys hurried ahead to the lovely little riverside village. Gladys watched anxiously for their return. At last she spotted the two figures returning on the little mountain path.

"Ai-weh-deh!" The boys seemed to be dragging their feet. Why were they coming back to the group, rather than waiting for them in the village?

"Ai-weh-deh!" As they approached, they shook their heads hopelessly. "Yuan Chu has been bombed. There is nothing left. No one is there. There is no food!"

Bombed! That meant the Japanese army was nearby, ready to march through the smouldering village with no opposition. Gladys fought down a wave of fear and disappointment.

"Well then," she said cheerily. "We will just have to go straight across the river!"

"But we can't!" the boys said. "There are no boats."

Gladys Despairs

Everything the boys had told Gladys was tragically true. When they reached Yuan Chu, little fires still burned in the debris. Thick smoke hovered over the village in ghostly patches. There was not a living soul to be seen. Gladys knew that if all the people had fled, that meant that Japanese soldiers were soon to arrive. Gladys couldn't bear to look at the fear and disappointment in the faces of the weary children.

"Come on, children! We'll find some nice trees by the river and rest there. The big boys and girls will go back to the village and look for food. There's bound to be a bit of grain left here and there. And we have the river! We'll make a nice soup!"

Gladys was surprised at how hoarse her voice sounded, and how desperately she was longing to rest. Still, there was nothing for them in the village. They would rest tonight, and tomorrow they would cross the river.

In the morning, the children were greatly refreshed, but Gladys still felt very tired. Her bones ached. Her head ached. But that was understandable after such a long journey. She tried to smile as Ninepence sat down beside her on the grassy river bank.

"How, honoured mother, can we cross the river?" Ninepence spoke softly and glanced cautiously at the children who had limped to the shallow bank of the river and were splashing and soaking their painful feet in the water. It wouldn't do to worry the children. "Mother, I have looked up and down the river, as far as I can see. There *are* no boats. There is a dock where there used to be a ferry to carry people across the river, but nothing is there."

"There is bound to be a boat now and then to take people across the river. We will wait. In the meantime, the children can wash in the river and you older girls can wash clothes. The hot sun will dry them in no time."

"I guess it's good that we can rest a bit." Ninepence tried not to show the fear she felt. "But mother, what if the Japanese soldiers come?"

Gladys closed her eyes. How good it felt to close her eyes. "God will protect us" she said sleepily. Noiselessly, Ninepence scrambled to her feet and made her way to the river. Mother was always right. God would protect us.

The first day spent at the river went quickly. There was thin soup to make, clothes to wash and the children played in the shallow water. But by nightfall, the children were tired and cold. Gladys had no answers for their insistent questions:

"When are we going to cross the river?"

"Why don't the boats come?"

"What will we eat in the morning?"

"Are the Japanese soldiers coming?"

"When the Japanese soldiers come, will they hurt us?"

Over and over the questions kept repeating. It was late when the children finally fell asleep. Gladys could not sleep. High above her, stars twinkled through the trees. A bright moon lit the sleeping clusters of children huddled together to keep warm. Thoughts and prayers spun around in her head. If the Japanese came, she would be shot as a spy. What would happen to the children? There was nowhere for them to go. If they tried to run away, they wouldn't survive alone in the mountains. What would happen to the older boys and girls? Gladys tried to fix her thoughts on Jesus. How He loved little children.

"Lord Jesus" she prayed, "these are your dear children. I have tried to save them. But now there is nowhere to go and the Japanese are coming at any moment. Lord, help us to get across the river. We must have a boat. Lord, don't let even one of these little ones perish."

But the next day came and went and there was no boat. Two days passed. Then three. The children were growing weaker by the day. There was an uneasy silence across the countryside. Everyone was straining to hear any sound that would signal that the Japanese were coming.

Finally on the fourth day, Sualan, one of the older girls came to Gladys. Gladys was sitting under a shady tree, trying the read her Bible.

"Ai-weh-deh, may I speak with you?"

"Certainly, Sualan. Come and sit down." Gladys patted the grass beside her.

"Ai-weh-deh," Sualan began when she was settled, "God parted the Red Sea for Moses and the children of Israel just walked across the sea to the other side."

"Yes, that is true." Gladys heart sank. She could tell what Sualan was going to say.

"Then why doesn't God part the waters of the Yellow River, and let us walk across?"

"I don't know, Sualan. But then, you have to remember, I am not Moses."

"But God is still God!"

Gladys was silent. A sense of terrible desperation came over her. Finally she said, "Shall we pray, Sualan, that God will get us across the Yellow River?"

Sualan got on her knees and folded her hands. Gladys stayed where she was. She wasn't sure she *could* move. As she began to pray, tears flowed down her cheeks. She had never known such despair. "I am finished, Lord. There's nothing I can do. We are going to die here, Lord. Why don't you help us? Did you bring us this far to let us die? Here is the river, but where are you? We have no food. We have no help. There is no boat to take us across the river." On and on she prayed. A few of the older children gathered around and joined Gladys and Sualan.

Finally, their prayers were interrupted by a shout from one of the boys, "Soldiers!" he yelled.

Panic shot through the groups of children. Sualan looked as though she might faint. What could they do? Gladys pushed her way up from the ground and hurried forward.

An officer strode his way toward Gladys. Her heart was hammering in her chest and she gathered up her courage for whatever was about to happen. She kept her head down, respectfully, and tried to breathe.

"Where did all these children come from?" The officer demanded. At the sound of his voice Gladys' head jerked up in astonishment He was speaking Chinese! He was a Chinese officer.

Gladys Escapes

Gladys bowed respectfully. "These are children from Yangcheng in Shansi province, honourable officer…"

The officer interrupted her. "Impossible! Where did these children come from! What are they doing here?"

"They are from the orphanage in Yangcheng. We walked across the mountains. We must get across the Yellow River."

"Impossible! The Nationalist Government has made a law: it is against that law for there to be any river traffic in these days. We are enforcing that order. You must get the children away from here. The Japanese will reach the river any day now."

From the corner of her eye Gladys could see the children clustering around the soldiers. They were giving them food from the packs they carried.

Gladys tried to keep the despair out of her voice. "Honourable officer," she said firmly, "we cannot go back. *That* is what is impossible. All the villages in this region are burned and deserted. Even if they were not, we can walk no further. We must get across the river." Gladys swayed a little on her feet. The officer led her to a fallen tree by the riverbank and helped her to sit down.

"It is against the law to cross the river. And even if there were to be a boat" he said quietly, "the Japanese air force patrols the river. If anything moves on the river, they swoop low and strafe the vessel with their machine guns. All the children would be killed or drowned."

Gladys felt a stab of hope. "*Is* there a boat?"

"We have some boats hidden along the bushes on the river banks. Only for soldiers. In case of an emergency. But as I said, it is suicide to use them."

Gladys clutched the officer's arm. "You *must* take us across. God will protect us from the Japanese planes. We must leave now. Right away! Never mind about the law. Where else can we go except cross the river?"

The officer stared at Gladys for a long minute. "It is madness!" he said as he got to his feet. Gladys was already hurrying toward the children.

"Children! Children! Come quickly. We are going to cross the river! The soldiers will help us!"

The soldiers looked very unwilling to help. They turned questioningly to the officer. "That's right," he said briskly. "Get the boats. We've got to get these children across the river."

The children were thrilled! None had ever been in a boat before. They clambered in, more than the boats could rightly hold. The boats tipped crazily.

"You must all sit perfectly still and keep the little ones in the middle of the boat. You must not talk or sing or move at all." The officer wondered for a moment if he should tell the children what to do if Japanese planes flew over. Then he decided against it. What good would it do? They would all be killed, no matter.

Into the river they went, in plain sight of any Japanese soldiers on lookout nearby and in plain sight of any planes. Gladys looked at the ragged little bodies filling the boats. They obediently sat as still as statues watching the bank recede behind them. The utter silence on the river frightened Gladys. "God," she prayed. "You couldn't have taken the children safely so far to have them die on the river!" She began to pray: "Oh, God, don't let the planes come! Oh God …" Then she stopped. What was the matter with her? *Of course* God would protect them. Hadn't He led them through the mountains? Hadn't He made a way across the river as surely as He had led Moses and the children of Israel through the Red Sea? Gladys closed her eyes and rested. She listened to the oars quickly dipping in and out of the water. She knew they would be safe.

What they hadn't expected on the other side of the river was the flood of refugees that seemed to pour out along the paths from the river toward the villages. Where had they all come from? Gladys had focused all her energy and prayers on getting across the Yellow River. She hadn't realized that reaching the orphanage at Sian meant another long journey. But here there was food and villagers eager to feed and rest refugees. Trains were still running, overflowing with refugees but no tickets were needed. When they could, they rode on trains and at last, walking all day from the last train drop-off, they saw the city of Sian in the distance. Throngs of refugees pushed around them, people excited to see the city of refuge.

Now all their troubles would be over! There would be clean beds and food and shelter for the children. Gladys would find somewhere to rest for a little, and then she would get to work helping in the orphanage. In such a big city, there would be much work to do!

"Children, when we march through the gates of Sian, let us sing! We will sing a hymn so that all the people there will know how great our God is, who brought us safely so far! What shall we sing?"

There were many suggestions but they settled on a well-loved chorus:

> *Trust and obey,*
> *for there's no other way*
> *To be happy in Jesus,*
> *but to trust and obey*

An old man by the roadside watched as Gladys and the children stopped for a few minutes to rest.

The children chattered excitedly about Sian and the wonderful things they would see in the great city. Monuments and ancient temples. Ancient tombs and markets selling wonderful food and many other things. They would sleep indoors and go to school again!

The old man hobbled over to Gladys. "Woman!" he said, "the wise adapt themselves to circumstances, as water moulds itself to the pitcher."

Gladys looked up at the old man. "Yes, grandfather. That is a wise saying."

"Daughter" he said, shaking his head slowly, his long beard wagging from side to side, "You will never enter Sian."

"And why not?"

The children close by were listening respectfully to the old man. "Because the gates stay closed. No more refugees are allowed in the city."

"This *can't* be true! We have come so far! We have come over the mountains on the other side of the Yellow River. We have come from Shansi provinces. They *must* let us in."

"You can continue on your way there, but they will not let you in. If what you say is true, you have lifted a very heavy stone." Gladys nodded. "Then you must have lifted it only to drop it on your own feet. It is useless for you to try to enter Sian."

"But what shall we do? Where can we go?"

The old man patted Gladys' head as if she were a child.

"Daughter, in Fufeng there is an orphanage. Many refugees find shelter there. In Fufeng the gates are not locked. There you can set down your heavy stone. There you must rest. You are ill. "

"I am *tired*," Gladys answered peevishly. Too tired to walk to Sian only to be told the gates are closed.

The old man gazed at the group of children. "So many children," he said sadly, almost to himself. "But still, the gates are closed."

Gladys could hardly bear to look at the disappointment on the children's faces.

Gladys painfully pulled herself up on her feet. "Then we find the train station and go on to Fufeng. Thank you, grandfather. May you eat your food in peace."

The old man nodded gravely.

Gladys closed her eyes in prayer and took a deep breath. "God help us," she prayed. "I have no strength left."

Gladys Is Victorious

Tears brimmed in Gladys' eyes as the village woman shouted excitedly. "No! No! There can be no train to Fufeng from here! All these children! You must go away! Our village can give the children some food. Then you must go away!"

Gladys was standing on train tracks. She could see the tiny station a short walk away. The children had gathered in sad little groups on the incline above the tracks. They were too exhausted to cry or to ask for food or to complain.

"But *why* is there no train? There should be a train here." Gladys pointed to the station.

The woman was old and dirty. Her padded jacket was torn and her eyeglasses smudged with dust. "Perhaps she doesn't know," Gladys thought. "Perhaps the war has affected her mind."

Three other women from the village were hurrying toward Gladys. "No train" they were calling. "The bridge is bombed." They were breathless as they stopped in front of Gladys. They stared at the children fearfully. "All these children…"

Now the tears spilled down Gladys' cheeks. "We *must* get to Fufeng. There is an orphanage there."

"The trains go from Tungkuah," one woman spoke gently, her eyes still on the piteous groups of children watching their discussion anxiously. "It is over that mountain." She pointed to a high mountain that rose majestically from behind the train station. "At Tungkuah there will be a train."

The youngest woman carried a large basket of food. She began passing small shrimp cakes and bread to the children until it was gone. Gladys wiped her wet face with a corner of her sleeve. "How long will it take us to get to Tungkuah?" The women were already making their way back to the village. One called over her shoulder. "Two or three days. Not more."

Gladys sat down on the tracks and began to weep. "I can't do it, Lord!" she sobbed. "Look at the children. *They* can't do it, either. We are finished. I have brought them all this way only to die. I have been stubborn all my life. I have been wilful. And now look at what I have done."

The children cried. The little ones hunched up as close as they could get to the older children and wailed. No one from the village came to comfort them. On and on they cried. After a time, Gladys stood up.

"All right, children. We've all had a good cry. Now we must go on. Gather up your things."

Slowly the children pulled themselves up. Some staggered on swollen feet. Older boys tried to carry the little ones. As they set off, Gladys forced her voice to be cheerful. "This mountain is going to be our very last mountain! I *promise!*" Her words echoed in her mind like prophetic doom. It would be their last mountain all right, if they didn't make it across. And if they did, no matter what was on the other side, they would be unable to walk one step further! "And we will come to villages on the way where we will find food."

"Our last mountain!" The children picked up the words and encouraged one another.

Gladys stumbled at the head of the weaving line of children. Sometimes she couldn't remember where she was or why they were all walking. Sometimes she thought she was in England or with Mrs Lawson at the Inn in Yangcheng. Soon the muleteers would be coming. "We have no fleas. We have no bugs! Good! Good!" she muttered.

When they came to little mountain hamlets, women brought them food and helped the children to find shelter in mountain caves or deserted temples. Gladys smiled, remembered to be polite, remembered to reassure the children. When they were walking, her mind was fixed on one thing: she insisted they keep going. The cries and suffering of the children were breaking her heart, but she felt she was floating above them all, her only task in the whole world was to keep urging the children forward.

Often verses from the Psalms would come to her. She walked in time with each word. "Yea … though … I … walk … through …the … valley … of … the … shadow … of … death …Thou … art … with … me …"

They came to Tungkuan suddenly, the curved roof of the train station shining in the morning sun. The bustle of activity assured them that there were trains.

Workers waited on the platform with shovels in their hands. "Shovels?" Gladys wondered. "Why would they have shovels?"

"Well, for the coal, old mother," one of the workers told her. *Old* Mother? Gladys had never been called "old" before. "These are coal transports that come through here. Only coal trains. One is due in late tonight."

"Then we will travel on top of the coal." Gladys did not hesitate a moment. "We must get to an orphanage at Fufeng."

In weeks to come, Gladys remembered only bits and pieces of what happened at the train station. The children slept until the train came. Then older children carried the sleeping little ones up onto the top of the coal as it gleamed in the bright moonlight in the open cars. The sleeping pads the children carried with them couldn't protect them from the sharp lumps of coal under them, but their exhaustion kept them sleeping. Gladys could recall the musty smell of the coal, the clatter of the train as it sped along the tracks, the bitter wind that whipped through their jackets until they shook with cold.

In the daytime they passed through lovely countryside, fragrant with fruit tree blossoms. Warmed by the sun, the children revived and cried out in pleasure at the sight of beautiful little shrines tucked into the sides of hills, wispy trees along small riverbanks, a grey crane, flying low, its harsh shrieks heard even over the clatter of the train. Gladys hardly saw the countryside. Her vision seemed blurred and she was only half-awake.

The coal train stopped at a large station where there were passenger trains. No tickets were needed as crowds of refugees packed into the train heading to Fufeng. Gladys hurried her flock into a large passenger car and tried to settle them quickly. None of the children had ridden on a train before, and they were excited and refreshed. How wonderful to travel sitting down! How lovely for there to be food to eat! They could sleep whenever they felt tired and they could run up and down the aisles in play when they wanted. They were perfectly safe from the weather and from the Japanese.

Gladys seemed to be sleeping all the time. The children brought her food and nudged her awake. She must eat a little. She must drink some water, then she could go back to sleep. Days and nights blurred into each other. How many days they were on this train, Gladys never knew.

Only she knew the wave of joy that thrilled her when they finally arrived, tired and dirty and hungry at the Christian refugee centre in Fufeng. Never mind that it was an old Buddhist temple that had been converted into a home for orphans and displaced children. Here the Shansi children would be given new clothes and shoes. They would be fed. Here would be school and games. They were safe. With God's help, she had done the impossible! She had brought one hundred children to safety from almost certain death at the hands of the Japanese! Not one had been lost.

"You will all be happy again!" she told them, "You must always, always remember what God has done for you!"

"But, Mother" Ninepence's sharp eyes saw that Gladys was preparing to leave. "Aren't you staying with us?"

"Two of the Bible women here, have asked me to go with them to preach at a meeting today. I will come back."

Ninepence saw the two women waiting patiently by the temple door. "Mother, you can't! You are tired, and sick."

"We have all eaten. I feel better. I will rest tonight." Gladys patted her daughter's hand. "Don't be worried. I came to China to preach the gospel. I must go."

The Bible women had heard of Ai-weh-deh. It would be wonderful to hear her preach! They chatted as they walked along. Gladys couldn't hear them. They should speak louder she thought, but it didn't matter. When they arrived at the hall the women hurried Gladys into the courtyard. There would be time for tea and, if she liked, a rest. Suddenly Gladys' feet seemed stuck. She couldn't move. There was buzzing. She waved her hand across her face to brush away whatever insect was bothering her, but the buzzing didn't stop. She squinted. For some reason it had become dark. She couldn't see. What a bother when she had to preach! Then darkness overtook her and she fell to the floor.

Gladys Has a New Beginning

After her collapse, Gladys was taken to a hospital run by Baptist missionaries. She was suffering from pneumonia, typhoid fever, exhaustion and malnutrition. She was so ill that for weeks doctors feared for her life. It took her six months to regain her health, but as soon as she was able, she gathered her adopted children and several others together and made a home for them in Fefung. But she needed money. Where would money come from for food and clothes for the growing children? Well, God would have to provide. Gladys and the children fervently prayed for His help and provision.

This time it was not a Mandarin who came to her rescue. It was the local Methodist church. Many missionaries had left China because of the war and the bitter persecution by the Chinese Communists. Many had been arrested and were imprisoned in concentration camps. The Methodists desperately needed workers to carry on their missionary and refugee work. "Would Gladys join them?" Gladys was thrilled at such a wonderful answer to prayer. "Of course she would!"

Gladys preached everywhere. Remembering the rioting men in the little prison in Yangcheng, Gladys found a great love for the inmates of the large Fufeng prison. Many became Christians, some just days before their tragic executions. In the overflowing refugee camps, Gladys started daily prayer groups so that her new converts could gain strength from older Christians. She preached in leper camps, hospitals, and to hundreds of troubled students at the local university. Her ministry with the students was amazing. More than two hundred students accepted Christ. Some of them became Christian martyrs, killed by the Communists because they would not give up their new-found faith.

Increasingly, as the war years passed, the situation for the Christians in Fufeng became more and more dangerous. Gladys' local fame was drawing angry attention from the officials. Her presence in Fufeng was bringing threats of death and imprisonment to the Christians.

On the advice of church leaders and elders it was decided that Gladys should leave Fefung and go to the great port city of Shanghai on the East China Sea. Although it was occupied by the Japanese, Gladys could more easily blend into the teeming population and escape attention. Besides, the elders pointed out, in the years since her great trek with the children over the mountains, she had never completely recovered her health. She needed medical attention and rest. Both would be available in Shanghai. Finally, Gladys agreed, not knowing that her life in Shanghai was to take an entirely surprising direction.

"What? Return to England? Me? Impossible!" Gladys stared at the Shanghai businessman in astonishment.

"China is my home! And I haven't a penny to my name for any such ticket! And I don't *want* to leave China. I want to live and die *in China!*"

The man smiled and bowed deeply in approval. "Of course. You will come back to China when the war is over. But for now, you must go. We in Shanghai cannot get you the doctors you need. And there is no rest here for you under the Japanese. And don't you wish to see your mother once more before she dies? And we can pay for your ticket to England." The arguments went on until Gladys came to see that it was God who had led her from Fufeng to Shanghai and who was leading her back to England.

On the journey home she began to daydream about what the future days would hold: she imagined quiet walks in the woods near home. Leisurely cups of tea with her mother. Hours of time to read her Bible and pray. Restful visits with Chinese Christians in London.

What she couldn't even begin to imagine was the fact that in England she was famous.

Her mother had been giving talks in churches all over London about "our Gladys in China." Sometimes Mrs Aylward read bits from Gladys' letters home. People who had never heard Mrs Aylward knew about Gladys from an article written about her by a British reporter who had seen her in China. The great British Broadcasting Corporation included the story of her escape over the mountains with one hundred children in a series on "war heroes." There was a radio play written about her life. Then there was a best-selling biography called, "The Small Woman." And last of all, a Hollywood movie was made with the international star, Ingrid Bergman, playing Gladys Aylward. It was an instant sensation. Now everyone knew the name, Gladys Aylward. She even met Queen Elizabeth, an amazing event, she joked, for an English parlour-maid!

True to form, Gladys used every minute of her fame to help China. She travelled all over Britain raising money for refugees, setting up collection centres for warm clothing for China, ministering to the floods of Chinese refugees who were entering Britain. To her now grown-up children in China, she wrote devotedly, and also carried on a lively correspondence with many of the children she had led over the mountains.

It broke her heart as she slowly accepted that she could never really return to her beloved Shansi. The Chinese Communists had been victorious in 1949 in their struggle to take over China. They would never allow the now-famous missionary, Gladys Aylward, to return. But Gladys was heartened to know she *could* go to Taiwan, the Chinese island nation one hundred miles off the coast of China. Although it was a province of China, it was not Communist, and Taiwan provided a haven for the former Chinese government and thousands of Chinese who had fled the Communist rule.

In 1957 Gladys said a final goodbye to her mother and set sail for Taiwan. There she worked in orphanages, taught the Bible and preached the gospel. She never stopped. She spent the next fourteen years of her life in Taiwan, grateful that God allowed her to carry on her ministry to the Chinese people. On New Year's Day, 1970, a newborn baby was brought to her flat in Taipei. The infant had been abandoned by its mother. Would Ai-weh-deh take it? Of course she would. She had everything she needed in her flat for the many babies that had spent time with her until a home could be found for them. She bathed and fed the little child and tucked it into the crib she kept in her bedroom. A New Year. A new baby. Gladys liked new beginnings. That night she fell asleep for the last time and awoke to a new beginning. She was in heaven.

Thinking Further Topics
Chapter 1
A Rich Man Asks a Question

What do you think about obeying orders? When is it right to obey orders and when isn't it? Can you think of orders that God has given us in the Bible? What was the name of the set of rules that God gave Moses? Can you think of other things that God has told us to do or not to do?

Gladys was a determined woman, strong-minded and sometimes stubborn. She didn't listen to people who told her to stay at home. She knew without a doubt that God had sent her to work for him in China. She wasn't going to disobey God's orders.

Gladys' boss told her to listen to those who were older and wiser than her. Do you think he was right to say that? Is someone who is older than you always wiser? What does it mean to be wise anyway? Can someone who is young or a child be wise?

Look up 1 Kings 3 to read a story about a young man, King Solomon, who was given a very important choice. God asked him to pick one thing: Long life, great riches or wisdom. What do you think he chose? What did he get?

What was one of the wise things that Gladys did? Look up Proverbs 11:30. This says that the person who wins souls is wise. How was Gladys winning souls, and who was she winning them for?

Answers and further discussion

- The Bible tells us that we have to obey our parents; respect employers and listen to what older and wiser people say to us. But God is ultimately in charge. The final authority rests with him. Following orders that go against God's law is wrong. Generally, following orders that would put yourself or others in danger is also wrong but many follow orders to go into dangerous places such as soldiers and fire crew.
- God gave Moses the ten commandments.
- Older does not necessarily mean wiser. Examples of young people in the Bible who were wiser than the older people around them are: Joseph who was wiser than his brothers; Daniel who was young but was promoted above the other wise men; Josiah who was eight years old when he was crowned King of Israel; Miriam who cleverly rescued her younger brother and Esther who became Queen of Persia and showed great wisdom in rescuing her people. Finally read Psalm 119:99.
- What does it mean to be wise? Read these Bible verses: James 3:13-18; Ephesians 5:15-20; Psalm 111:10, 1 Corinthians 1:17-25.
- Remember that wisdom is a gift from God. Anyone who trusts in God can have wisdom if they just ask God for it. James 1:5.
- Solomon chose wisdom and God gave him long life, great riches and wisdom!
- Gladys won souls for God, by preaching the good news of Jesus Christ, and the free offer of salvation from sin that is offered to us through his death on the cross.

Chapter 2
Gladys has a Daring Escape

Gladys thought she knew the value of prayer but when she was in real trouble she realised that prayer was even more important than what she had thought.

Is prayer important to you? What does prayer give you? Does prayer give anything to God? Does He need to hear from you? Does He want to hear from you? At what times can you pray? Is there a special way in which you have to pray? What is prayer, anyway? Is there more to it than asking for things? When you are communicating with God what other things should we talk about, in addition to requests for help? Is prayer only for when you're in trouble, or should you pray at other times too?

Stop and think about the dangers you face on a daily basis. Isn't it amazing that God protects us all the time. Sometimes we won't even realise that we are in danger. Just because you haven't seen danger or felt fear doesn't mean that God hasn't protected you. Think about times when you may not have realised that you were in danger.

And another amazing thing – God often answers prayers before we even ask them. As you read Gladys story, think about this fact that God answers prayers before we even think of asking them. God could be doing the same thing in your life just at this moment.

Answers and further discussion

- Prayer should be an important part of your life. Prayer is a direct line to God where you can take your troubles to Him and ask Him for help in many different situations.
- It is also a way to repent and say sorry to God for your sin. It is where you can tell God that you love Him and are thankful for what He has done for you.
- God may not need to hear from you but He certainly wants you to communicate with Him.
- You can pray at any time and in any way – though you should remember who you are talking to and show respect and love.
- There is more to prayer than asking for things and we must show love and repentance and thankfulness in our prayers. If you were to communicate with someone just to ask them for things your relationship would be very selfish and one-sided.
- The Bible actually says that we should pray without ceasing. So prayer should be an ever present and important part of our day. We can pray in a classroom as much as we can pray in a church and we can pray while eating a hamburger or cycling a bike – and we don't need to shut our eyes when doing it!

Chapter 3
Gladys Arrives in China

Gladys must have been very disappointed when she realised that instead of arriving at her destination she still had another 100 miles to travel! ... and on foot! How do you deal with disappointment? Gladys wanted to cry. Some people sulk and others completely lose their tempers. What is the best thing to do when you're disappointed and feeling down? When you feel depressed, do you talk about it to someone or keep it to yourself?

Gladys began to feel more and more concerned about her situation and was overjoyed when it turned out that she was going to get a guide to help her. What might have happened to Gladys if she had not been given a guide to take her to Mrs Lawson? What generally happens when people travel in an area that they don't know, without a guide? What should they have done?

In what way is your life like a journey? How is your life like the journey that Gladys had to make? What provisions do you have to help you on your travels through life? Who has given you these provisions?

Read the following verses and discuss; Psalm 22:1-11 and then verse 22-24.

Answers and further discussion

- Thanking God for the good things He has done helps us focus on the positive rather than the problems. It is a mistake to turn to alcohol or drugs to deal with problems or depression. These things always make things worse – even legal things like shopping or eating chocolate to get you out of a bad mood is not always a good idea. Turn to God and ask Him to help you focus on the hope that He gives in His Word, the Bible.
- If Gladys hadn't had a guide she could have got lost; wandered into danger and got hurt. People who get lost often don't have a guide or even a map. They aren't prepared. Life is like a journey because you are travelling from the day of your birth to the day of your death. When you die you must be ready for heaven. You must trust in Jesus who died to save you from your sins. Be prepared for the journey of life by trusting in Jesus Christ and focusing on his Word.
- Our life is like Gladys' journey because it is dangerous and full of problems. But God has provided salvation for us and instructions and advice in His Word, the Bible. He also gives us friends, family, a conscience and common sense to use along the way.
- Psalm 22:1-11 was written by someone who had problems. But he took his problems to God; he promised to tell others about how amazing God was (verse 22) and in verses 23-24 he tells people how God has listened to his prayer and answered him. This psalm starts off with someone who is wondering if God even exists but in the end, once he has spoken to God, he realises that God is listening and is wonderful and that even the future is taken care of (verse 31).

Chapter 4
Gladys Bursts into Tears

Gladys had expectations of China and of the woman that she would work for. She was looking forward to the adventure and the challenge but the problems were harder than she had expected. When Gladys arrived at Yangcheng it looked beautiful on the outside and as she drew near she must have been thrilled to experience the sights and sounds of the real China. But Gladys discovered a different situation once she was inside. What did the native Chinese do when they met her? Can you think of times when you have assumed that something or someone is wonderful but then you've discovered that you were mistaken?

God's Word says that people look on the outside when they look at other people but God looks at the heart. If you could look into someone's heart what would you want to find out about them? When God looks into someone's heart what does He see? What is it that really pleases God?

Gladys' plan was to tell the Chinese about Jesus Christ. Do you sometimes imagine what your life is going to be like? Do you think about the perfect boyfriend or girlfriend, the perfect school report, the perfect job, the perfect car – and what your life would be like if you had these things? Perhaps you are planning to be a missionary just like Gladys or perhaps you plan just to be good and work hard and then everything will be alright? What are your plans for your life? What might happen to these plans of yours? Can you depend on your dreams or not? Who or what can you always depend on?

Answers and further discussion

- The Chinese people threw mud at Gladys and called her a foreign devil. When God looks at a person's heart he sees everything – their emotions, thoughts, aspirations, dreams. He can see all the secret things you keep to yourself. He can see if you love him or if you don't really care about him at all.

- Read the following verses for some answers about how to please God: Psalm 69:30-31; Psalm 147:10-11; Proverbs 15:8; Colossians 3:20; 1 Timothy 2:1-4; Hebrews 11:6.

- If you are only making plans for tomorrow and the next day and are not making plans for eternity then you are not really prepared for the most important event of your life. When we die we must be ready to meet with God. When we meet with God, and Jesus is with us, we are accepted by God the Father because of what Jesus, God the Son, did for us on the cross.

- Our plans can be stopped and changed in an instant and without our say so. Your plans might succeed but God is ultimately in control. Sometimes our plans do not succeed simply because we are living in a difficult and changing world. Though Gladys got a cold and unfriendly welcome in her new home, and her journey had seen one problem after another, Gladys knew that she could always depend on God. He is the only one that we can always depend on. Matthew 28:20.

Chapter 5
Gladys Terrifies a Mule

Gladys found the reality of missionary life quite a surprise!
What would you find the most difficult thing to cope with
as a missionary like Gladys? Would it be the language or
the long journey or being away from your family? Perhaps
it would be the fleas?

What had Gladys thought would be her first words in
Chinese when she became a missionary? But instead of these
what were the first words that she actually learnt?

Are there things in your life that you never thought you
would have the courage to do? Have you ever surprised
yourself by succeeding at something?

What do you think success means? Who would you pick
as an example of a really successful person? Would you pick
someone who was rich, or talented or beautiful or clever?
Perhaps you think someone who is successful is someone
who is very popular? What problems can you see for each
of these successes? Are any of them lasting?

When God is looking for someone to do a special job
for Him, what characteristic is the most important in His
eyes?

Can you think of people in the Bible who were successful?
What helped them to reach success?

Answers and further discussion

- Gladys thought her first words in Chinese would be "Jesus loves you." Instead they were "We have no fleas!"

- Success can be physical, i.e. how much money you earn, or spiritual, i.e. how much you honour God, how much you learn about Him and how much you are obeying and loving Him.

- Rich: Money can be lost; it doesn't bring lasting happiness and when you die it means nothing.

- Talent: This is something that you can lose. When you grow old you may not be fit enough to be a star sportsman. People may change their minds and say you aren't talented after all. You can also misuse your talent by using it just for yourself and not for God.

- Beauty: This is something that fades with time and is only skin deep. Real beauty is spiritual. If your heart loves God that is real beauty.

- Clever: If you are clever and know lots of things but don't know that you're a sinner and that Jesus is the Saviour – then you don't know the most important thing.

- Popularity: People are fickle and change their minds. There is only one who you can depend on for all eternity: Jesus Christ. None of these successes are lasting. God looks on the heart and the most important thing is that your heart belongs to him.

- Moses was not a good speaker but God chose him to go against Pharaoh to set the Israelites free. David was a small shepherd boy who defeated a large giant. God helped them both. You can probably think of many other examples.

139

Chapter 6
Gladys Meets a Mandarin

Mrs Lawson was not patient with Gladys, even though it was difficult for Gladys when she was starting a new job, in a new country and in a new language.

But everybody has faults. Mrs Lawson had a temper with a short fuse. What kind of things make you lose your temper? Do you lose it quickly? Do you say something in the heat of the moment and regret it afterwards? When you lose your temper can you think what parts of your body are involved? What is the best way to control your temper? Can you think of practical things which might help? What good idea does God give us in Ephesians 4:26? One particular part of the body that is used when we are angry is mentioned in James chapter 3. This talks about taming our tongues. How is your tongue like a wild animal or a forest fire?

Mrs Lawson and Gladys were both stubborn. But God loves his people despite their faults. There is a verse in the Bible that says God uses the foolish things of this world to shame the wise. What do you think that this verse might mean?

Even though we make mistakes, God loves us. He wants us to keep going and to do better next time. God loved you even before you loved Him and He wants you to enjoy this love and to tell the world about Him and His greatness. What things do you consider to be great about God?

Despite their faults Gladys and Mrs Lawson gave their lives to spread the good news of Jesus Christ. They made a good choice.

Answers and further discussion

- Temper: Lots of parts of our body are involved when we lose our temper. We see or hear something and then lash out with words or actions. One practical thing that the Bible says about anger is: "Do not let the sun go down while you are still angry and do not give the devil a foothold." Ephesians 4:26-27. This means that if you fall out with someone you should sort it out as soon as possible. Don't go to bed before saying sorry to someone when you have lost your temper, because if you don't you are letting the devil win.

- In James chapter 3 it talks about taming our tongue, which is like a wild animal as it has to be restrained before it causes damage. Have you heard of the analogy of a bull in a china shop? The bull would cause a lot of damage – so does a tongue that is undisciplined. This is not just in anger however – as gossip and lies can cause just as much damage. The tongue is also like a forest fire. Forest fires cause damage the world over. They are also dangerous. The words that we say in the heat of the moment can hurt people, and destroy lives and relationships, so they are also damaging and dangerous.

- God uses people with abilities in his work but he also uses people with faults or who don't have fantastic gifts. He used Gladys who was a poor parlour-maid and was not well educated. He used her in order to tell Chinese people about Jesus. But Gladys had a heart of love for God and a desire to save souls. God used her to show more clever and more successful people that it is God who is the most important and he is the one that matters.

Chapter 7
Gladys Unbinds a Tiny Foot

The practice of foot binding was very painful for the babies and girls who had to go through it. It meant that the older Chinese woman had deformed feet. People thought that small feet were more beautiful for a woman. This is an example of people causing physical harm in order to appear physically attractive to others.

What other harmful things do people do in order to be more attractive? When God sees a person what does He look at and what do people look at?

You can do things that are harmful to your body and soul such as food and alcohol abuse and drugs in order to make your body a particular shape or so that you look cooler in front of your friends. But once you start it is very difficult to stop. You can become addicted and even though it is destroying you, it can be too hard to stop it.

It is hard not to do what everyone else is doing. There is nothing wrong in belonging to a group or looking good as long as what you do is healthy and what God wants. God has created your body and given it to you to look after. In what ways can you look after this precious gift on a daily basis? Is it just your flesh bones and blood that you have to look after? What other part of you has God given?

When you think of people who have fallen into drug and alcohol abuse think about how their lives have been destroyed. List the ways that these things harm and destroy people. Think about Jesus Christ now, who loves you and wants the best for you. Make a list of the things that Jesus wants you to have.

Answers and further discussion

- Other harmful things people do to be more attractive. Smoking; getting drunk; crash dieting; drug abuse. These can harm and sometimes kill the person involved. Some can lead to mental as well as physical health problems and disease. Crash dieting can lead to eating disorders. If you or a close friend are involved in any of these things, you need to ask for help.

- In order to appear attractive to the opposite sex, young people can become involved in sexual relations outside of marriage. They are afraid that if they don't they will be laughed at. There is a lot of pressure to have sex outside of marriage today, but this is against God's law. It causes emotional hurt as well as unwanted pregnancy and disease.

- When God sees a person, what does He look at and what do people look at? People look on the outward appearance but God looks on the heart.

- You also have a soul to look after as well as your body. This is the eternal part of you that lives for ever. You must accept Jesus Christ as your Saviour, in order for him to save your soul and give you eternal life in heaven, with him, when you die.

- Drug and alcohol abuse destroy your health, your looks, your relationships and friendships. They can make you dangerous to be with, they can get you in trouble with the police, and they can even kill you or make you kill someone else.

- Jesus wants you to have abundant life on earth, eternal life when you die, great joy, forgiveness, fulfilment, peace and a loving relationship with God.

Chapter 8
Gladys Gets a New Name

Gladys had to ask herself a question as she waited outside the prison. "Was God God, or not?" If she chose to stay outside the prison it would have shown that her faith in God was poor and perhaps people would have thought that this God she trusted in was not as powerful as she lead people to believe. People would have doubted Gladys' faith but they would also have doubted her God. However, Gladys chose to trust in God and she went into the prison. What situations in life can make you scared? Do you ever feel as if you're not in control of your life or of yourself?

Do you believe that God is God and that He is in control? What happens when things go really wrong? Does this mean that God has lost control? Why does God let these bad things happen?

Perhaps you want to believe in God but you have so many questions? Questions are not wrong. If you have them you should ask them, and ask God to help you understand. Don't feel bad about not feeling absolutely sure about things. People in the Bible had huge questions and doubts. But remember that it's not about how great a faith you have, but it is about having faith in a great God.

Ask God to help you show others how powerful He is by trusting Him in every difficult situation.

Answers and further discussion

- Problems, grief, death, tragedy, why does God let them happen? This is difficult to answer when someone is in great pain, or has lost a loved one. Sometimes God lets things happen because He is the only one who can see from the very beginning to the very end of this world and beyond. He knows everything and knows that what is good for someone may be painful. Something heartbreaking can happen to you, and years later you look back and can see how God completely changed you from that day on. You may still wish that it had never happened but you realise that God's plan for your life meant that these painful things had to happen.

- When things go wrong it doesn't mean that God has lost control. It's because of sin that the world is in chaos. Humanity turned away from God and from His perfect plan and as a result death and chaos are part of life. Though sometimes God lets bad things happen for a special reason, mostly these things happen because a world that turns its back on God is a world that has chosen to go its own way. That way means that instead of living in a world of love and peace, we are living in a world of hate and fear.

- So instead of asking God why He lets bad things happen we should wonder why He has given us so many good things like love, friendships, beauty, freedom and the great gift of salvation through Jesus Christ. These are gifts we will never deserve but God still loves humanity and He wants to show it.

Chapter 9
Gladys Becomes a Mother

Gladys hated the poverty and injustice that she came across. She did what she could and made it her business to help where others were either too frightened or too poor to do anything. Why is it easier to ignore poverty and hardship? Why is that wrong? What does Jesus say about helping the poor and standing up for justice? Matthew 25:31-40. Look up the following story in the Bible: Luke 10:25-37. Which of the people in this story is Gladys most like?

When Gladys rescued the little girl she gave her two names, "Ninepence" and "Beautiful Grace". Why did Gladys give her the first name? Perhaps she gave her the second name because the little girl was beautiful and graceful, or because she had a beautiful and graceful nature.

If your friends were to make up a new name for you, what words would they use to describe you?

Some people say that it is important to see ourselves in the way that others see us. Sometimes we can be grumpy and unpleasant but we don't realise it – it's only the people that we spend time with who see us as we really are. Sometimes when we are out with people that we don't know very well, we put on a good show and are very nice and everyone thinks we are great. But when we are at home we don't put in so much of an effort. God is someone who is with us all of the time and sees us always. What do you think God sees when He looks at you?

Answers and further discussion

- It is easier to ignore poverty and hardship because if we don't ignore it then we have to do something about it and that can be very hard work. But although it is easier to ignore it – it is far better to be active and doing something to help. This is what Jesus did – He cared for the crowds of people He met everyday and He did what He could for them. He fed 5,000 people one day and He healed many men, women and children from illness and disease.

- We don't hear of Jesus giving money to people – He wasn't wealthy. What other things can you give to help people other than money? Time, love, help.

- It is wrong to ignore poverty – that is a selfish attitude. Look up these verses to find out what the Bible says about poverty and action: Psalm 34:6; Psalm 35:10; Psalm 140:12; Isaiah 25:4.

- If you give food, drink, clothes, friendship to those who are needy it is as though you were giving these things to Jesus himself.

- Gladys is most like the Good Samaritan.

- If you trust and love the Lord Jesus Christ, when God looks at you, it is Jesus Christ that He sees. He sees Christ's perfection which covers all your sins.

Chapter 10
Bombs Fall on Yangcheng

Gladys lived in a dangerous time in the land of China – and her opinion was that this was why she really had to focus on preaching the gospel. It was the good news of Jesus Christ that she had come to tell the Chinese about.

Can you draw comparisons between Gladys' time and today. Are we living in dangerous times? What have you heard of recently on the news that tells you this? Do you feel that there is more fear in your world than there was a year ago or two years ago? What do you think you should do about fear? The Bible says that perfect love casts out fear. Would you say that you have perfect love? Do you love anyone perfectly? Who does have perfect love?

When you think about the emotion of fear can you think of practical things that would help you to get over it?

What does the Bible say about fear? In Psalm 23:4 it mentions something that is scary. What is that? Then it goes onto talk about how you can gain comfort. How do you get that comfort? What profession is being described in this psalm? And how does this job involve protecting things? In what way does God behave in a protecting way?

Answers and further discussion

- Don't give into fear; trust in God; love him; believe in His love for you and his power.
- Perfect love is seen in Jesus Christ who died for us on the cross to save us from our sins.
- Practical things to combat fear: taking your mind of things; being reasonable and thinking things through; praying; talking to someone about it.
- Psalm 23:4 talks about death and how with God we don't need to fear any evil. He gives us comfort because He protects us in the same way that a shepherd protects his sheep. A shepherd protects his sheep from wild animals who would harm and kill; he makes sure his sheep have plenty to eat and drink, a safe place to sleep and that otherwise they are fit and healthy. God protects us in many ways on a day to day basis. Many times we don't realise that He has done this for us – but we should always thank Him for his love and care of us. He protects our souls. If we trust in Him and love Him our souls will go to heaven after we die. Death is a reality but so is heaven for those who trust in Jesus Christ. God provides for us too. He provides for our physical needs: food; clothes etc. as well as our spiritual needs: salvation; forgiveness; learning about God from His Word.

Chapter 11
Gladys is Astonished

Gladys' life in China was taken up with providing and caring for others and it was through her words and actions that she introduced the Chinese people in her area to the one who really cared – Jesus Christ.

What effect do your words and actions have on the people around you? What do your friends think about the way you behave? If you're a Christian do the people you spend time with know this? Do they know this because you have told them, or because they know you go to church or because your actions are different to everyone elses? Words and actions are both important – especially for Christians. You can say that you follow God and are a Christian but if you don't show this by obeying God, then your words don't mean a thing.

In your opinion what can cause more harm – words or actions? How can your words show Jesus Christ to people? How can your actions show Jesus Christ to people?

The Mandarin came to believe that Jesus Christ loved China and he saw this first of all because Gladys loved China. Does God love your country? Look up John 3:16. In what ways has he shown his love to your country specifically in the past? Does your country love God? How would you decide if a country was one that loved and honoured God? John 14:15.

In what one particular way did God show His love for all of humanity? In the Bible it says that there is one love that is greater than other loves. What is it? Look up John 15:13.

Answers and further discussion

- Words can harm when they cause hurt; spread lies or gossip; tell untruths; bring dishonour to God's name.
- Actions can hurt in physical and emotional ways – injury; abuse; fear; distress. As a Christian your actions are important. Non-Christians look at the actions of someone who says they love God. If your actions are hurtful or wrong people can get the wrong idea about God. Instead we should be focusing on what Jesus would do in all situations.
- Your words can show Jesus Christ when you
a) explain God's Word the Bible to someone and tell them the good news of Jesus Christ,
b) when you speak with love and compassion to someone,
c) when your words are good and pure and honouring to God.
- Your actions can show Jesus Christ to people when you show mercy and love and obey God's Word like Jesus did.
- For God so loved the World – He loves all tribes and nations and languages.
- If you love God you will obey his commands. Does your country obey God's commands?
- God showed His love for all humanity by sending His son, Jesus Christ, to die on the cross for our sins. The Bible says that there is no greater love than that someone died to save his friends. Jesus Christ did this.

Chapter 12
Gladys Becomes a Spy

Many people throughout history have made decisions that are controversial. Many people today would say that war is wrong. They are called pacifists. Gladys however did not adopt this opinion and during the war she joined forces with the Chinese. How is it that a pacifist and someone who is fighting in a war can both be Christians and followers of Jesus?

In the Bible you will come across people who did controversial things. Queen Esther who was a Jewish woman married a heathen king. Jesus Christ healed people on the Sabbath and did other things on God's day which annoyed the religious people. One day Jesus was so angry with the greed that was shown in the temple of the Lord in Jerusalem he overthrew some of the tables which belonged to the money changers. Another time he was hit and spat on by Roman soldiers but he didn't do anything to stop them.

What kind of difficult decisions do you think you might have to make one day? Is there always right and wrong decisions for something?

You will find that in your life different situations demand different actions but that God and His Word are always there as your guide.

Answers and further discussion

- God has said that murder is wrong; yet he helped David and others to fight against their enemies. This shows there is a difference between the sin of murder and fighting in a battle. However war and death are situations that arose because of humanity's disobedience against God. It is important to defend your country but there have been times when war was wrong. The Bible promises us that there will be a time when wars and fighting will cease. Look up Isaiah 2:4.

- Jesus kept God's law perfectly. He was sinless. Even in his anger He did not sin. He was right to show this anger to those who defiled the temple of God with their greed. But he never showed selfish anger as we might do if we were hurt or upset. Jesus Christ did everything perfectly. His actions were exactly what was needed for that particular time.

- You may have to make difficult decisions about jobs; marriage; children etc. If you read God's Word and pray for His help and guidance He will show you what decisions He wants you to make. When there are specific instructions from God's Word He will direct you to them when you read it or He will bring them to your memory. That is why it is a good idea to do some scripture memorisation.

- For some decisions there are no right or wrong answers… such as what job to do or what college course to take. God can guide you in this too, but sometimes we should just ask God to be with us and help us to honour Him in whatever job or college course we chose to do.

Chapter 13
Gladys Falls in Love

Gladys fought against her love for Linnan. In later years there was a little mystery about her relationship as she was never very open about it with other people. But other books and sources have shown that this relationship did exist. It must have been a very exciting, but anxious time for Gladys as she tried to decide what was the best thing to do.

Do you think it is possible for someone to choose to fall in love, or even to choose not to fall in love or is it something that just happens? Do people have control over this sort of emotion?

What sort of guidance or advice does the Bible give about choosing someone to marry? The following verses can be read in different ways but one way you can read it is that it is God telling us about who you should not marry. 2 Corinthians 6:14-15. Why would it be a problem for someone who loves God to marry someone who doesn't? Do you think you should just follow your heart when you are choosing a boyfriend/girlfriend or husband/wife? Can you think of ways in which it is wrong just to follow your heart and ways in which it is right?

Is it possible to be a missionary and make God the most important person in your life and then also to fall in love with someone else at the same time?

Answers and further discussion

- If you read 2 Corinthians 6:14-15 in such a way that it is giving you advice about marriage, then it is telling you that if you love and follow Jesus Christ you should not marry someone who does not feel the same way about Christ as you do. Believers should not marry unbelievers. The Bible mentions other things about relationships between men and women such as – do not commit adultery; be the husband of one wife; love your husband; love your wife.

- Following your heart can be good. If our hearts are right with God and we are trusting in Him then He can guide our emotions as well as our thoughts. Jesus showed compassion and love and so must we. Following our heart can be bad though, as sometimes we can let our emotions run out of control. We must remember that we still have to struggle against sin and our hearts can make us want to do wrong things. It is good to do things and make decisions using both our minds and our emotions and to always ask God for His help and advice.

- It is possible to be a missionary and to love a husband and wife at the same time. It's just the same for a missionary as it is for any Christian. God is pleased to put people into families, and to give them loving friendships and relationships which honour him. Just because you are in love or married to someone doesn't mean that God isn't first in your life.

Chapter 14
Gladys Becomes a Fugitive

Gladys was conscious of a guidance in her life at dangerous and difficult times. Have you ever felt that God has guided you at specific times of your life? Are you always aware of God working in your life?

At what times in Gladys' life did she come across danger and then discover that God had provided a way out? God spoke to Gladys at different times in her life and in different ways. He does the same with us today.

How does God speak to us through His Word, the Bible? How does God speak to you through your conscience? On rare and special occasions what other ways can God use to communicate with people?

Find out about Joseph (Genesis 37) and Samuel (1 Samuel 3) and Daniel (Daniel 10) and Joseph the husband of Mary (Matthew 1). In what special ways did he speak to these four people. Now find out about Gideon (Judges 6); Zechariah (Luke 1); Mary (Luke 1). In what special way did God speak to these people?

It is amazing to realise that if Gladys had not been amongst the first people out of the gates that morning she and the other people with her would have been killed along with the soldiers and other refugees. Gladys wasn't aware that God was actually telling her to get out she just had a feeling. She sensed that something was wrong. God can speak to us in so many different ways – we should pray that he will guide us and help us to realise when he is speaking to us.

Answers and further discussion

- You are not always aware of God working in your life. It can sometimes be years later when you look back at what happened that you realise that God was guiding you and helping you, but you weren't aware of it at the time.

- Gladys was also rescued in Russia when she was going to be forcibly detained to work as a machinest under the communist regime. She was provided with a rescuer who helped her get to a boat and to safety.

- God speaks to us through the Bible by giving us instructions; rules; advice; comfort; guidance; love and forgiveness.

- God speaks to us through our conscience – by giving us an uncomfortable feeling when we are doing something wrong; giving us a strong conviction when we know we should or shouldn't do something. However, if you aren't reading God's Word and following Him, praying and asking Him for guidance and help your conscience may not be strong and as a result you may not realise when an action is wrong. If you start to ignore your conscience it will also stop working for you.

- Dreams and angels are sometimes used to communicate with people. Sometimes God speaks to our hearts but in Samuel's case He spoke audibly.

- Joseph; Samuel; Daniel and Joseph the husband of Mary were all spoken to by God through dreams.

- Gideon; Zechariah; Mary and her husband Joseph were all spoken to by God through angels.

Chapter 15
Gladys Makes a Decision

Gladys had to make a very painful decision. She loved Linnan but this relationship was getting in the way of their duties. What was Gladys' first and primary duty? Who had to be first in her life? What would have happened if she had married Linnan at that time?

How does God help us to make decisions? What has He given you in order to help you do this?
If your heart was telling you do one thing and your conscience was telling you to do another what would you do? How would it make you feel?

Have you ever had to make a decision which was really difficult? Can you think of some practical things to do when you are trying to make an important decision?

In the Bible we read about people who had to make difficult decisions but they did so because God guided them. Abraham left his home; Gideon had to fight the Midianites; Ruth had to leave her country and family; Esther had to marry a foreign king; Hannah left her child, Samuel, behind to be a worker at the temple. Some people in the Bible made wrong decisions – Peter denied Jesus Christ; Judas betrayed him; David committed adultery. We should ask God to help us make the right decisions and to show us what he wants us to do.

Answers and further discussion

- Gladys' first and primary duty was to God and to the spreading of the good news of Jesus Christ.
- If she had married Linnan she was worried that they would both forget what their duties were – that he would want to keep her safe and so stop her doing what she was supposed to do – reach out to the Chinese with the gospel and be with these people and help them. And that Linnan would stop doing what he was supposed to do which was being a soldier.
- God helps us make decisions by giving us His Word, the Bible, so that we know what rules God has given us and how He wants us to behave, He has also given us minds so that we can think things through as well as other people we can ask advice from.
- When making an important decision it is good to pray; it is good to ask advice from friends and family or people we trust; it is good to ask advice from someone who might know some information about your problem or situation; sometimes it is good to relax or to sleep on things and then get up fresh the next morning and make the decision then.

Chapter 16
Gladys Begins her Epic Journey

Gladys was never finished with making decisions. She was always having to decide what to do next, how to avoid the Japanese and how to get herself and others to safety. Instead of the decisions getting any easier they seemed to get harder as things went on.

She had decided to say goodbye to Linnan and now other people were asking her to say goodbye to China. They were telling her that she should leave the people that she loved in order to get to safety.

But Gladys was determined to make the right decision. God had called her to China. She knew that without a doubt. So as far as she was concerned, there were only two options to live in China or to die there. She was so certain about God's call to her she even agreed to pray about it but was sure that there would only be one outcome. Gladys wouldn't think of doing anything but remaining where she was – in China – the country that God had brought her to.

Was it right for Gladys to think in this way? In what ways was it wrong to think like this? In what ways was it right?

Gladys was ready and willing to leave things up to God, but in one way she had already made up her mind. She didn't think that God's plans for her might be different.

Do you have plans for your life? Perhaps you have good and sensible plans for your future? There is nothing wrong with that, but what does this part of Gladys' story and the following chapters teach us?

Answers and further discussion

- It was wrong for Gladys to think that she could pray to God about something and that God wouldn't change her plans. She was assuming that God's plans were her plans and that she could pray and that God would follow along with what she had decided. It is possible for God to lead you in one direction in your life and then to lead you in another direction. Just because one thing was right for you to do last month or last year doesn't mean to say that it is what God is wanting you to do this week.

- However it was right for Gladys to stand her ground when people were saying that she should flee for her own safety. Her motives were certainly right. She didn't want to put herself first before the other Chinese or before God's will for her life. She felt called to preach the gospel to the Chinese. What she didn't realise was that God had other plans. These plans involved Gladys saving others from danger and not just herself and then later going to preach the gospel to Chinese people in another land… Taiwan.

- This part of Gladys' story and the following chapters teach us that we can't assume that we always know what God wants us to do. God sometimes has surprises for us.

Chapter 17
Gladys Has a Problem

Gladys' firm decision to stay where she was, was soon turned on its head. She had been certain that God's call to China had meant that she should stay there for the rest of her life. However this wasn't God's plan. How did God tell Gladys what he wanted her to do?

When Gladys was praying to God for guidance she poured out her heart to the Lord. What do you think this means? Is it an easy thing to share troubles and problems with God. Do you tell God about the things that you think about and feel in your heart? Do you tell Him about the good times and thank Him for them? Do you tell Him about the things that break your heart? It is important to be honest with God when you speak to Him and to tell Him exactly what you feel. It is useless to try and hide things from God as He knows it all anyway. When you are honest with God and tell Him what is on your heart, it is a good way to sort things out and to find out if you are following God's ways or not.

Jesus had emotions too. In the Bible we hear about when he was angry, when he was sad and wept and when he showed compassion. Jesus also felt lonely when the disciples left him and he had to face his enemies alone.

Answers and further discussion

- God told Gladys what to do when she was reading His Word, the Bible.
- Pouring out your heart. This is a picture of someone pouring out the contents of a jug or bottle. If you are pouring something out — you are taking what is hidden inside the bottle or container and then bringing it out. Pouring out your heart is similar — it is taking the heartache and the joys from inside and showing them to someone, talking to someone about them, praying to God about them.
- It isn't always an easy thing to share the feelings in our heart with God, especially if we are ashamed of them. But God is loving and forgiving and will forgive us for our mistakes and wrong doing if we say sorry and truly mean it.

Chapter 18
Gladys Despairs

Gladys was in great difficulty and danger. With so many children to look after, and the Japanese army not far away, all seemed lost. Gladys could have looked after herself and left on her own for China when she was given the opportunity, but she would not leave the Chinese people she loved so much. The only way she would leave the country was in order to save the lives of all these children. But things were incredibly difficult for Gladys as the journey got harder and things started to get on top of her, and then with success and freedom in sight it all started to slip away.

What do you do when things get on top of you and you feel as though you just can't go on? When you feel down and in a bad mood what do you do to get yourself out of it? Gladys was so down that she seemed to forget who was in charge. What Bible miracle did Sualan remind Gladys of when she was feeling so depressed? Why did Gladys think that this miracle would not happen to them?

But God was still God, and a miracle of a different sort was just about to happen. When Gladys saw a soldier she didn't expect him to be Chinese! But he was! Often when we are in trouble and pray to God he can provide answers for us that we don't expect. Sometimes these answers are better than we ever imagined. God is amazing and He answers us in amazing and totally unexpected ways.

Answers and further discussion

- Tips for getting out of a bad mood: punch a pillow for three minutes; go for a walk; get to bed earlier; eat healthy foods; listen to some music; have a sharing time with a friend. Talk to God about it.

- The Bible miracle that Sualan reminded Gladys of was when the Israelites crossed the Red Sea and Moses stretched out his arms and the sea split in two allowing the Israelites to cross the ocean on dry land. Gladys made the mistake of saying that that miracle happened to Moses a long time ago and that it was different today. But Sualan reminded her that the God who helped Moses was still in charge, and was the same God that Gladys loved and worshipped.

- If you look up this chapter you will discover a story about a group of Christians who had been praying for someone. Do you think they were expecting God to answer their prayer? Acts 12:1-18.

Chapter 19
Gladys Escapes

The river crossing was a success but then more problems arose for Gladys and the children. However, on their journey they sang a chorus which has a valuable lesson to teach us in situations like this! What was it called?

What does it mean to trust someone? What does it mean to trust God and to obey him? What do we get when we do this?

What did Gladys do when she realised that the city was shut and that instead of being at the end of the journey there was still a long way to go?

With no strength left Gladys had only one person that she could turn to – God.

Gladys must have gone through so many emotions on the epic journey into free China. She felt fear, despair, hope and then despair again. She would have been exhausted physically and emotionally. Jesus also understands what it is like to go through physical and emotional exhaustion. Look up the following scriptures: Matthew 4:2; Mark 4:38; John 19:28 Matthew 11:28. What do these tell us about Jesus Christ?

Answers and further discussion

- Trust and obey.
- Trust means believing in someone, loving them and respecting them. You know that you can depend on them.
- Trusting and obeying God means that you know you can depend on Him because He is faithful and He loves you. You also love Him and respect Him. You know that whatever He tells you to do is for your own good and for His glory.
- In the chorus it says that if we trust and obey – there is no other way to be happy in Jesus but to trust and obey. If you are not trusting and obeying God then you will not have the joy of salvation that is available through Jesus Christ and His death on the cross.
- The Bible verses tell us that Jesus was hungry; tired and thirsty – physical feelings that we all have. Matthew 11:28 tells us that he is concerned about us when we are tired and weary. He tells us that we can come to Him with our troubles as He understands and He loves us.

Chapter 20
Gladys is Victorious

With God's help Gladys had done the impossible! She rescued over 100 children from the Japanese army and took them through a battle zone into free China.

What things in your life and in your world seem impossible to change? Is there a country or a situation that you think is always going to be a mess, where there is always going to be famine and fighting and disaster? Perhaps there are things at home or school that are bothering you. Read Psalm 46 and then look up these verses to get a different perspective on things: 1 Corinthians 1:25; Isaiah 55:8-9; Ephesians 3:20-21.

There have been many problems and battles in the Bible for God's people – but he helped them. Gideon's army was tiny in comparison to the Midianite enemy – but with God beside them they defeated them soundly. Remember that God sometimes chooses to help people in impossible situations in order to show them and others that he is in control.

If Gladys Aylward, who was a parlour-maid in London, could manage to be part of a miracle that took 100 children through a battle zone to safety, then anything can happen. It seemed as though there wasn't a mountain that was too high for Gladys to climb. She managed to travel on her own to China, she learnt a new language, became friends with a mandarin and stopped a prison riot. She did all this because throughout it all God was still God. You too can change your life, your country and even your world. If you ask for the same help that she had – God's, whatever mountain you try to climb, you will climb it with his faithful help.

Answers and further discussion

- Remember that God can turn things on their heads and in Psalm 46 we hear that he can turn wars into peace and even break spears and bows and other things that are the equipment of war. Today there are lots of wars across the globe and we can find it disturbing and discouraging as we hear of yet another conflict. We can pray, though, to God about our world and we can trust him. What he has done in the past he can do again today and in the future. It is interesting to know that the wisdom and strength of the human race is nothing in comparison to God's wisdom and strength. His ways and his thoughts are much better than ours, and we can rely on God to provide us with what we need. He can do so much more for us than we can even imagine.

- Jesus said that even if you have faith as small as a grain of mustard seed you will be able to move a mountain. (Matthew 17:20). There can be mountains of all sorts in our lives – mountains of problems, heartache and sadness, difficulties, hard decisions, illness. Think about the problems in your life, the problems that seem like mountains to you that you can't seem to get over. Think about how Gladys managed it and think about how with a little faith in a great God you can accomplish wonderful things. Don't let these mountains stop you. With God you can move mountains!

Chapter 21
Gladys has a New Beginning

Gladys' life was full of changes and adventures and new beginnings. She started off as a parlour-maid and became a traveller. She almost became a prisoner and a machinist in Russia and then she became an inn worker. Later on she was in charge of unbinding the feet of baby girls and was an evangelist. She fell in love and became a spy. She rescued 100 children from the Japanese army but never went back to China again.

Gladys had been called by God to China where she thought she would spend the rest of her life. But God had other plans. However, these changes were all part of God's guidance in Gladys' life. In her controversial energetic life Gladys was certain of one person – God. Her life had changed dramatically, but her God had never changed. He was always there.

What changes do you think your life is going to bring? Imagine what you might be doing 30, 50 or 60 years from now.

Gladys was born in 1903 and by the time she died in 1970 the world had changed dramatically. Can you think of some changes that happened in that time frame? But who remained the same? Yesterday, today and forever the Lord Jesus Christ is Lord and Saviour.

Gladys always knew this, though she sometimes had to be reminded of it. God was still God. He was God for Moses when he crossed the Red Sea, and He was God for Gladys when she crossed the Yellow River, and He was still her God when it was time for her to cross the final barrier between herself and heaven. And He is still the same God for you.

Answers and further discussion

- Of course we can't tell what we might be doing years from now. It may be that God has other plans that we aren't thinking about. Quite often we don't think that we are going to die – but we will – so we should be prepared for that.

- Gladys was part of a century that saw changes in technology, communications, medicine, fashion and morals. Gladys was born at a time when to communicate with another country you had to write a letter. Telephones were the new invention. By the time she died people were just beginning to realise what computers could do. Today we have mobile phones; e-mail; internet; satellites. Gladys was born before the days of antibiotics. Penicillin was only discovered in 1928. Today we have many new cures and medicines available to help combat disease. Perhaps some of the biggest changes have been in people's behaviour. One of the things that happened in Gladys Aylward's life time was that in the United Kingdom and the U.S.A. women were able to vote for the first time. This happened in 1928 in the U.K. and in 1920 in the United States. Times have changed during the last 100 years for good and bad – but God is the same for ever.

- What things in your life would you change if you could start again from scratch? Remember that spiritually God is willing to give us all a fresh start. If we turn our lives over to him, asking for forgiveness for our sins – he can wipe us clean because of what his Son Jesus Christ did on the cross. This is the new beginning that we all need.

Time Line
Gladys Aylward

1902	Gladys Aylward was born.
1904	The Trans-Siberian Railway completed.
1907	First electric washing machine introduced.
1909	Plastic invented.
1911	The Chinese Revolution.
1912	*The Titanic* sank.
1914	World War I began.
1918	World War I ended.
1924	First Olympic Winter Games.
1927	BBC founded.
1928	Penicillin discovered.
	Gladys Aylward rejected by China Inland Mission.
1931	Empire State Building completed.
1932	Gladys Aylward sets out for China by Trans-Siberian Railway.
1934	The introduction of 'apartheid' in South Africa.
1936	Gladys Aylward became a Chinese citizen.
1937	Japan invades China.
1938	Japanese planes bombed Yancheng.
	Gladys Aylward trekked to safety across the mountains with 100 children.

1939	World War II began.
1940	Gladys Aylward is wounded by Japanese soldiers.
	Winston Churchill became Prime Minister.
1941	Japanese attacked Pearl Harbour.
1944	Ballpoint pens go on sale.
	D-Day.
1945	First computer built.
	World War II ended.
1947	Gladys Aylward returned to England for a badly needed operation.
1948	State of Israel founded.
1949	China became Communist.
1951	Colour television introduced.
1952	Elizabeth II became Queen.
1953	Gladys Aylward founded an orphanage in Taiwan.
1957	Alan Burgess wrote a book about Gladys Aylward called "The Small Woman".
1958	NASA founded.
1961	Berlin Wall erected.
	Soviets launch first man into space.
1969	Great Britain abolished the death penalty.
1970	Gladys Aylward died.

Lilias Trotter: Daring in the Desert
by Irene Howat

'You could become the greatest living painter. Your paintings would be treasured for ever.' Those were the words Lilias Trotter heard from John Ruskin, one of the world's most established art critics. She had to make a choice between her talent and her calling. Both were gifts from God. In May 1879, Lilias knew what she should do. God's work for Lilias was in the desert land of Algeria. Palm trees and camels replaced lampposts and horse drawn carriages. The desert was her home, its people her friends and its Creator her reason for life.

ISBN: 978-1-78191-777-0

OTHER BOOKS IN THE
TRAILBLAZERS SERIES

For a full list of Trailblazers, please see our
website: www.christianfocus.com
All Trailblazers are available as e-books

CHRISTIAN FOCUS PUBLICATIONS

Christian Focus | Christian Heritage | CF4K | Mentor

Christian Focus Publications publishes books for adults and children under its four main imprints: Christian Focus, CF4K, Mentor and Christian Heritage. Our books reflect our conviction that God's Word is reliable and Jesus is the way to know him, and live for ever with him.

Our children's publication list includes a Sunday School curriculum that covers pre-school to early teens, and puzzle and activity books. We also publish personal and family devotional titles, biographies and inspirational stories that children will love.

If you are looking for quality Bible teaching for children then we have an excellent range of Bible stories and age-specific theological books.

From pre-school board books to teenage apologetics, we have it covered!

Find us at our web page:
www.christianfocus.com

CF4·K
Because you're never too young to know Jesus